Hello There, Target Guests!

I'm Rachel Hollis and if we've never met, let me tell you there's only two things you need to know. First, the Dollar Spot can and *will* entertain your toddler for a solid forty-five minutes while you slowly follow them around sipping your Starbuck's cold brew and killing the hours until naptime. And second, I'm married to Dave Hollis (the author of the book you're holding in your hands). Our friends at Target asked if I'd write an opening letter for his book, and since I love this store (seriously, I'm probably following a toddler around the Dollar Spot right now!) and I love my husband . . . here we are.

When you're asked to write a letter like this, you have an amazing opportunity to say just about anything. For a hot minute I considered creating a three-page novella about a vampire falling in love with a librarian (or something equally as romantic), but that's much more for me than it would be for you. So fine. Allow me to utilize the next couple of pages to offer some advice that I think you might find helpful.

Many times in the pages of *Get Out of Your Own Way*, Dave references hard conversations we've had over the years. He and I have spoken about these times openly and honestly on our podcast *Rise Together*, but inevitably I still get questions: *How do I have a hard conversation with my partner without it turning into a full-scale fight? How do you talk about what's bothering you without them becoming defensive? How do you discuss sensitive subjects so that you come to a resolution instead of building more resentment?*

Well, friends, the big guy and I have been married for fifteen years (almost sixteen by the time this book makes its way to you), so I can tell you that we both have loads of experience trudging our way through hard topics together. So here it is, my best advice (earned through trial and error) and I hope it helps you the next time you have to talk to someone you love about something that's hard.

1. **Pray and meditate on it—for a while!** Right here at the top, you're maybe going to roll your eyes. Telling someone to pray or meditate on a conversation sounds like advice you've heard ten thousand times before, like drinking water or getting eight hours of sleep so you can function like a normal human being. It's like, *Jeez, tell us something we don't know!* Seriously, though, I know you've heard it a lot, but the reason you have is that it's good advice. The thing is, the worst arguments we've ever had in our marriage were when I tried to talk through a BIG conversation in the heat of the moment. You know those conversations, right? It starts out being about someone needing to unload the dishwasher and turns into a big, crazy blowout about that one time he hurt your feelings three years ago. Rather than getting into a fight that doesn't actually lead you anywhere, take some time—a lot of time— to think through what you want to discuss and what kind of resolution you're hoping for. When Dave and I have had to talk through really difficult things, I've had to fight against my nonconfrontational nature to wade into the thick of it. To do that, I prayed my way through what to say and how to say it for days, weeks, or months in advance. Taking the time to think it through also allows you to align your thoughts and ensure that you're able to clearly communicate the way you're feeling.

2. **Practice.** Okay, I don't know if other people do this, but whenever I have to talk through something rough, I absolutely practice the conversation when I'm alone in my car. I started doing this years ago for whenever I needed to be candid with someone on my team at work. As a leader, it gave me the chance to organize what I wanted to say. By saying it out loud you're able to listen for how it might sound and whether it fits with your intent. It worked so well for me at work that I started doing it at home too. This was really powerful, because I tend to shut down in confrontation and if I've practiced I'm less likely to skip something, even if it's hard to say.

3. **Say it in a way that they can hear it.** Having a hard conversation isn't just about talking or speaking your piece. The only reason to have a hard conversation is so that you can improve your relationship—otherwise it's just arguing for the sake of arguing. So, before you even begin you have to ask yourself a very important question: *How can I present this in a way that* they *can hear it?* Dave is—bless his heart—a wee bit defensive. Okay, more than a wee bit. So if I rush to make a point or don't think through the conversation he will go fully into a defensive mode and can't really receive anything I'm saying. This doesn't serve either one of us. I find that if I start with my intent and my hoped-for outcome right at the top (rather than the problem I'm having), then we're both on the same side working through a problem, and it always ends up so much better.

4. **Be honest, but kind.** If you're going to wade in to a tough conversation, have the courage to be truly honest. If you're not honest it's just going to keep festering and growing and you'll never move past it. So be honest. Explain your opinion

by owning it rather than making sweeping generalizations. For instance, by saying "I feel like" or "To me it seems that," you're qualifying that this is how *you feel*, not necessarily how they are. In all of that honesty, though, be kind. This is someone you care about and love—we don't intentionally hurt people we love, not ever. Your words have the power to lift someone up or tear them down, so be thoughtful with how you use them.

I hope these ideas are helpful or at least give you some food for thought. Remember, everything that you want to be good at (your life, your career, your parenting style, your relationships) are going to require effort. Lots of effort. Regularly and for the rest of time. It's such a pain to have to get into tough conversations but you come out the other side so much stronger and better, ready to take on the world together. Thanks for taking the time to read my advice and thanks for grabbing a copy of my best friend's first book. We both hope you love it!

xo, Rach

PRAISE FOR *GET OUT OF YOUR OWN WAY*

"In *Get Out of Your Own Way*, my friend Dave has identified an important truth: believing certain lies about ourselves keeps us skeptical that we can ever change the trajectory of our lives. Thank goodness in this great book Dave also shares with us the tools that helped him change his own life so you can change yours too."

—John C. Maxwell, *New York Times* bestselling
author and leadership expert

"*Get Out of Your Own Way* is a testament to one's ability to take control of your own life by freeing yourself from the lies that hold us back. Dave's approach to max out his life will inspire readers to do the same!"

—Ed Mylett, entrepreneur, bestselling author,
speaker, and top podcast host

"In his compelling first book, my friend Dave Hollis shares his path to change with candor, humor, and humility in a way that will inspire you to take charge, change your habits, and lay a foundation for living the life you always dreamed of."

—Lewis Howes, *New York Times* bestselling author
and host of *The School of Greatness*

"Dave's uncommon life experience of catapulting to the top of the corporate world, then going against the norm and quitting to run he and his wife's business to staggering success makes him uniquely qualified to write this amazing book. A book that anyone looking to take their life, career, income, and happiness to the next level must read."

—Dean Graziosi, *New York Times* bestselling
author, entrepreneur, and investor

"Through sharing his own sometimes rocky path to change his life, Dave Hollis encourages, inspires, and motivates readers to set aside their own demons and dream big, so that they can live their best life."

—Amy Purdy, *New York Times* bestselling author,
athlete, and motivational speaker

"Through compassion, wisdom, self-deprecation, and by his own account, learning the hard way at times, Dave is a master at taking life's hardballs and turning them into valuable tools that will absolutely change your life if you let them!"

—Heidi Powell, transformation specialist from ABC's *Extreme Weight
Loss*, entrepreneur, and *New York Times* bestselling author

"Dave Hollis delivers a straightforward, no-B.S. approach on how to overcome the barriers we put in our own way towards the life we were meant to live."

—Gary John Bishop, *New York Times* bestselling author

"You can feel uncomfortable about asking for help, or you can grow. In *Get Out of Your Own Way*, Dave Hollis brings a fresh, candid take on what it takes to truly live your best life by sharing his personal journey of pain and growth. I loved the book. It moved me and it will move you. Your bigger future is front of you. Get this book, read it, and get going again!"

—David Bach, *New York Times* bestselling author of *Smart Couple Finish Rich*, *Smart Women Finish Rich*, and *The Latte Factor*

"Have you ever picked up a book and found yourself immersed in pages you feel were written for you to read? While Dave may have written this from his perspective as a man, it's equally insightful and inspiring for women to dive into! I laughed, got a little teary, and walked away with a new understanding of how to bring my own gifts to the table and how to honor others who do the same."

—Jenna Kutcher, entrepreneur, digital education guru, and host of *The Goal Digger* podcast

"You'll be hard-pressed to find another of book of its kind with more candor, insight, and life-changing information than *Get Out of Your Own Way* by my friend Dave Hollis. He is one of the most successful people I know, and I commend his bravery in baring his soul to help others achieve their best lives."

—DeVon Franklin, Hollywood producer and bestselling author

"*Get Out of Your Own Way* speaks to anyone who needs a road map to reaching their fullest potential. In revealing the ways many inadvertently sabotage their own success, he offers invaluable strategies that will help you take control of your own life and make the world respect your greatness."

—Trent Shelton, author, motivational speaker, and founder of Rehab Time

"Take a chance on yourself! This book is a call to action for everyone to think and live differently. Dave inspires readers to show up for their lives today so that they can live their best life without regrets."

—Jesse Itzler, entrepreneur, author, and speaker

"*Get Out of Your Own Way* is the wakeup call we all need to do something to change our lives for the better."

—Colin O'Brady, world-record holding explorer, author, and speaker

GET OUT
OF YOUR OWN
WAY

A SKEPTIC'S GUIDE TO GROWTH AND FULFILLMENT

DAVE HOLLIS

HARPERCOLLINS
LEADERSHIP

AN IMPRINT OF HARPERCOLLINS

Published by HarperCollins Leadership, an imprint of HarperCollins Focus LLC.

Any internet addresses, phone numbers, or company or product information printed in this book are offered as a resource and are not intended in any way to be or to imply an endorsement by HarperCollins Leadership, nor does HarperCollins Leadership vouch for the existence, content, or services of these sites, phone numbers, companies, or products beyond the life of this book.

ISBN 978-1-4002-1543-0 (eBook)
ISBN 978-1-4002-1542-3 (HC)
ISBN 978-1-4002-2081-6 (IE)
ISBN 978-1-4002-2338-1 (signed)
ISBN 978-1-4041-1303-9 (custom)

Library of Congress Control Number: 2019953527

Printed in the United States of America
20 21 22 23 24   LSC   10 9 8 7 6 5 4 3 2 1

For Rachel, in gratitude for how your example of embracing growth and reaching for more taught me the value of doing the same.

CONTENTS

IS SELF–HELP FOR BROKEN PEOPLE?

I drank a handle of vodka.

In a day and a half.

By myself.

While I was supposed to be watching my kids.

Hello. I know what you're thinking. *What's a "handle" of vodka?* That's not your first thought? Well, I'll tell you anyway. It's that pitcher they sell at Costco—59.2 fluid ounces or roughly forty shots. I drank all the vodka. All. Of. It. Dad of the year.

After working in entertainment for the last two decades in stints that saw me as a tour manager for Beyoncé when she was still a Destiny's Child, launching TV shows for Fox, managing celebrity talent at an agency, and, most recently, working a seventeen-year gig at Disney as the head of sales for the film studio, I hit bottom. Despite being married to my best friend and having four healthy kids, the nice house, and the fast car, I found myself feeling stuck. Struggling.

Reaching the low point all started when we decided to go on our most ambitious vacation ever. (Yes, I'm going to be that guy who complains about a vacation.) We rented a house for longer than we ever had before—twelve days in Hawaii—grabbed our four kids ages nine, eight, four, and four months (we are idiots), and took off for paradise.

On the flight I was handed the near-final Word-doc version of my wife's new book *Girl, Wash Your Face*, getting my first glimpse into just how transparent and vulnerable Rachel had decided to be—and, in a vanity-alarm-bells kind of way, just how many of my deepest insecurities would be exposed and how much of this *everything's-great-trust-me* veneer I'd worked so hard to maintain would be challenged by her work.

Also on that first day of our trip, Rachel got sick—and by that I mean demons-have-inhabited-her-body, should-we-go-to-the-ER, let's-set-up-the-quarantine-from-*E.T.* kind of sick. So I did what any good dad and husband would do. I left her to rest, called for a sitter to come take care of the baby, grabbed this book of hers, and made a drink to enjoy by the pool while the boys played. My plan seemed so good.

In a way that I now see as divine, this was a combo platter for the ages: a personal funk running into its second year, me being in my early days of therapy (more on that in a second), the decision to read a book that would trigger many of the insecurities that lived and breathed in the funk and the therapy, all while having a few drinks—my issue-avoidance specialty at this point.

It was a perfect storm.

I got to chapter 5, the one that paints a less-than-ideal picture of our early years and casts me in a light I'm not proud of, and I poured less soda with the vodka when I made the next drink. By the time I got to the chapter about how much we struggled in our sex life, I stopped pouring soda at all.

We were at the beginning of a twelve-day vacation, and though Rachel got better on day three, I never recovered. I withdrew even more than I had already withdrawn. I got up in the morning, put on headphones, and went on a long run. When I came back from that run, I kept those headphones on, and, against the picturesque backdrop of Hawaiian perfection, turned on a baseball video game I'd brought and shut myself inside with another drink while my family enjoyed the beachfront view. I showed up like an ass for the entirety of that vacation, spiraling to the lowest point of the valley I'd been heading down for quite some time.

Rachel loves to explore a new place, and one morning, when she suggested she was excited to explore the island and hit the farmer's market, I told her I was going to "just chill at the house." That look on her face haunts my dreams. I want to make a joke about it here, but, honestly, I'm sad for that dude not showing up for something so simple. It's embarrassing. It sucked. I knew it in the midst of it, knew it on the flight home, and really knew it when we got back to our house and had *the talk*.

There will be a handful of moments you look back on that fundamentally changed your life—when you met your partner, your decision to take a job that ended up propelling you forward, things like that. This *talk*, this decision we made—that my wife made—to wade into and have a hard, hard conversation about the trajectory of our lives, that was one of those moments for me.

The day after Hawaii, we sat on our bed and Rachel worked against every ounce of muscle memory in her being. We're both recovering codependents and confrontation on this scale isn't something either of us had mastered, but the stakes were too high to worry about that. This was going down. She laid it out in such simple terms, but those terms rocked me to my core.

"I'm going to reach for a better version of myself every day. I'm going to do it whether you decide to do it or not. Personal growth is one of the most important values in my life, so I'm going to pursue it every single day. Are you going to choose to grow every day, or are you going to tread water? If you aren't growing and I am, in three months, will we have as much to talk about on date night? In six months, will we still make out as often? In a year, will we still be going on dates? In three years, will we still be married?"

Dagger. To. The. Heart.

Someone should have yelled "clear" before she hit me with the paddles to the chest, it was that fast. Through a pool of I'm-embarrassed-I'm-sobbing-this-much tears, I realized it was up to me to make a choice. Did I want to grow, or did I want to die? Did I want to rise to the level of who I knew I could be? Who God made me to be? Did I want to have an exceptional marriage, be a present father?

Of course I did. I always had. I'd lost my way, but now I knew it more clearly than ever. I knew it because, for the first time, I'd been forced to visualize the possible future that would result from my inaction. The future that sat in front of me if I didn't take this seriously, if I didn't take massive action to change what I was doing—or not doing. And here's the thing: even though our most likely scenario was a world where I didn't make changes and simply lived in a marriage where we drifted apart, I still forced myself to imagine the absolute worst case, in vivid detail, because I needed the leverage of the most brutal things I could think of to get my ass off the mat. Not having my best friend by my side. Switching weekends with who had the kids once we separated. Continuing to withdraw without my right hand there to hold up a mirror. I saw the overweight, unshaven, barely sober, lonely version of myself that could be if I didn't snap out of whatever it was that was holding me down.

It made me sad. It made me angry.

I felt shame and disappointment.

It was just the thing I needed.

As the kids say, I was shook.

Pain can be incredible leverage. The possibility of underutilizing your potential can be incredible leverage. So can brutal, obvious truth. The idea that you could be more but got in your own way should wake you up in the middle of the night. The idea that you could have been more and might look back at the end of your life with regret should be the single greatest motivator you can tap into.

It seems cavalier to say that I didn't ever think about me and Rachel getting divorced—I honestly hadn't—and I'm going to bet that most people don't give a ton of thought to it before they find themselves past a point of no return and wake up to see they've become *irreconcilable*. The notion of "irreconcilable differences" as a rationale for divorce was something I'd heard about but never given much thought to. It frankly seemed like a convenient term for people who didn't want to work hard enough on staying together. How naive of me. When I'm honest, it's clear now that we were in the earliest stages of a path that leads down that irreconcilable road, where a couple doesn't know each other anymore, doesn't share the same set of values for their life or their relationship. By grace, we were wading into confrontation while reconciliation was still something we could accomplish together.

Don't get me wrong. I'd been a good husband and father, but I'd careened into a slump that threatened everything I'd built, everything we'd built. And, to put a finer point on it, I'd been "good," but my family deserved "great." I'd been "good," and they deserved "exceptional." That vision of my future where I'm not as close to my wife and kids—that created urgency.

It forced hard conversations with my wife.

It required some difficult looks in the mirror.

Desperate-times-desperate-measures kind of stuff.

And it opened me up to "personal development" as a thing I might need to get out of that rut.

I could puke just thinking about it.

Before I tell you what happened next, let's rewind a few months before Hawaii when Rachel took her entire team to a four-day personal-development conference—a full-on immersion with all the music and fanfare. She'd been spending more and more time reading books about personal growth and was excited for what the opportunity to grow her team might look like at an event like this. I didn't get it. I didn't get the books she'd been reading or the impulse to attend a conference, so I eye-rolled behind her back and left her to live her best life (while I continued the descent into my worst). I was suspicious of this kind of event and these kinds of teachers. I honestly thought they were charlatans, peddling feel-good mysticism to weak souls.

If I'm totally truthful, I worried she'd come back talking about this cool cult we had to join. *Fortunately for me, it was way worse.*

My wife came back on fire. She wanted to jump around and do all these inside-baseball things that only people who'd been kidnapped for four days knew about, and this thing I didn't understand turned into this thing I didn't like. I didn't like that she was on fire. It's a terrible thing to think, but I didn't. Not because I didn't want her to be her very best self, but because it exaggerated the distance between her now new-and-better self and where I was. That contrast felt worse than it ever had.

She started waking up at 5:00 a.m. to get a jump start on the day, write her books, get her exercise in, and do all the things before the kids were awake. 5:00 a.m. *Every morning.*

What was in that Kool-Aid? I figured it would wear off, but it didn't. In a move I give her credit for now, even though it really frustrated me (which I expressed with my exaggerated grunts when I'd roll over as she got up), she never stopped. She made a decision to keep doing what she knew was going to make her a better person tomorrow, and she did it even though it was bugging the crap out of me. That choice—the decision to unapologetically reach for a better version of herself—had an effect on me over time. What started as anger (obviously, in hindsight, *fueled by my insecurity that she might outgrow me* if she continued to evolve) slowly gave way to curiosity.

What the heck has gotten into her?

How is she still so motivated?

How can she keep doing so much better when I seem to be doing so much worse?

I had no clear answers. I was struggling to know where to begin. I'd been able to figure things out on my own for so long that it was hard to admit I might actually need help to get out of this muck I felt stuck in. At this point, I started to ask questions.

I was finally willing to address this space between who I was and who I wanted to be—this space between Rachel growing and me dying. It was a catalyst for me to take a first step toward therapy.

"The best way out, is always through."[1] Poet Robert Frost is one of few influences from college that I'll still quote today. As it turned out, I had to get into it and work through it if I was going to be able to get out of it. Dang it, Robert Frost.

So, now, a few months removed from her team revival and about a month before vodka-ville in Hawaii, I started my time on a couch. For me, getting unstuck took a lot of hard conversations and even more work. I learned how exhausting it is pretending like everything's great when it isn't. I learned that, as much as it *is* possible to change your life for the better, before any of that can happen, you have to dig into what is keeping you from a more exceptional life in the first place. You have to do the hard work of identifying and acknowledging the stories you tell yourself that control your life and keep you running in place.

Starting therapy is hard. You're picking at scabs or looking at scars, maybe for the first time in a long time. Many of them are from long ago but maybe haven't totally been dealt with or healed.

It's a bit raw.

You're making yourself vulnerable.

I'm doing a terrible job selling therapy.

But honestly, it's work before it's extraordinary. I was in the work phase.

I had an unfavorable outlook on this whole idea of therapy. I mean, if I went to the gym, I'd tell everyone I knew about it, probably complain about how sore I was to remind everyone that I went. I'd even post videos of me swinging the battle ropes on Instagram to make sure my being at the gym was known to all. But therapy? I couldn't imagine bragging about therapy. I felt sorry for people who needed therapy. There's shame wrapped up in needing it. At least there was for me.

Who needs therapy? Before I went, I was positive I knew the answer. Crazy people. Weak people. Broken people. People who don't have supportive people in their lives. Women (ladies reading this, I was a caveman then). *Not men.*

So much of what was holding me back at the time came from how I (and I think most of us) grew up believing men were "supposed to be." How I showed up as a husband, father, employee, human—so much was connected in some way to societal expectations, either how manhood was modeled for me or how being a man was taught to me by the world around me. This collection of experiences laid a foundation for how to be, telling me the type of "manliness" society calls for and defining masculinity according to the models from my youth.

This was an ideal I chased but never quite achieved. I'm the son of a contractor, and I can't nail two boards together to save my life. I don't know how to hunt or fish. I cry even thinking about the end of *Rudy*. Does that make me the right or the wrong kind of man?

Ironically, the one thing I thought I knew about being a man was that real men had their lives together. Real men didn't need help. Real men certainly didn't need to spend an hour a week with a counselor.

News flash: That's total crap. It just is. It's a lie based on expectations that have been reinforced generation to generation and hardwired into our brains. *Failure makes us weak,* or *It's on us men to fix everything,* or *Vulnerability is for soft people.* All are ideas we need to challenge (and I will in this book). I needed an interruption to my regularly scheduled programming, a departure from what this society dictates as right and wrong. I needed a tune-up.

If the warning light on your car comes on, you take it to a mechanic to get the car checked out. Well, the warning lights in my life had been flashing, and I'd been breaking the warning lights rather than finding a mechanic. I broke them by regressing into a lesser version of myself and muting the things (do I dare call them feelings?) bubbling up that I didn't like—with headphones, long runs, full drinks, video games, and every other form of withdrawal.

I'd become so good at pushing away my feelings that I didn't have a handle on what was actually wrong. This conversation on a couch, facilitated by a stranger whose only job was objectivity and lending an ear, rebuilt the warning-light systems I'd broken and gave me a fighting chance at addressing what was keeping me from the sense of fulfillment I was in search of.

Here's the truth: You can stick to your guns and keep believing that "real men don't . . . ," or you can be fulfilled. You can feel uncomfortable about asking for help, or you can grow. You can feel strange about letting your guard down and becoming vulnerable (*gasp*), or you can connect with the people you love on a level that actually matters.

So I got over myself and saw a therapist. And it was good. Yes, it was freaking weird and uncomfortable at first. I felt dread when I knew I was heading in, and I stumbled at first at being honest and open. I had to get into a rhythm, out of my head, and past the worry of what other people might think if they knew. And then, a couple of sessions in, when I wasn't paying attention, therapy was suddenly no longer a negative thing. I even started looking forward to it. It was a space where I could sit with someone who didn't judge me, didn't correct me, didn't try to explain things, and frankly didn't even really try to help fix anything (at least at the beginning). She listened, asked the right questions, and sat back as I threw up all the crap I'd been struggling with.

What did we get into on that couch? The big questions that came up as I was crossing a crazy bridge, the bridge that is going from your thirties to your forties. This is an interesting season for a man. At least it was for this man. Twenty to forty had more or less gone as my twenty-year-old self had imagined, but at some point, I started asking questions. Those big, existential questions you only usually ask at milestone birthdays—though this time they didn't last for just the birthday week.

What am I on this planet for?

What does it all mean?

Is this really as good as it gets?

What was the meaning of the last episode of Lost?

Okay, there is no answer to the last question, but the others were coming up on a loop. That loop was running at a time when I'd *stopped growing.* I didn't identify that at the time, but, looking back, the absence of growth lining up with my milestone fortieth birthday was a catalyst for a spectacular meltdown.

I never thought the midlife crisis was a legitimate thing. For me it was a thing. A gnarly, batten-down-the-hatches kind of thing that wasn't fun as it unfolded but that produced some extraordinary fruit. I mean, yes, it prompted me to ridiculously invest a couple of years and way too much money into a 1969 Bronco that we now affectionally call the Incredible Hulk, but, on a deeper level, the experience of going into that valley is something I'm grateful for because of how it changed the way I think about *growth*. Now that I'm climbing out, I realize I'm climbing something that doesn't have a peak. I appreciate that I'm on a never-ending growth journey.

Therapy softened the soil. It took a thing that was taboo, turned it on its head, and became a negative-turned-positive. It opened me up to considering that there could be something for me in this personal-development space.

As it turned out, Rachel bought us tickets for a personal-growth conference before we went to Hawaii. I had just started going to therapy, was wading into my muck, and, against my better judgment, I said yes to a thing that I knew had worked well for her but that I was still unbelievably skeptical could work for me. I did it to make her happy. It still felt cheesy and cultish and, in some strange way, an affront to the idea that church and the faith I grew up in were enough to make me whole—like seeking out a teacher who wasn't a pastor somehow marginalized my beliefs. Plus, I believed the stigma that self-help was for broken people.

When I think about it now, it doesn't make a ton of sense. This stigma that existed in my mind, or in society generally, didn't apply to all men in all spaces. The greatest athletes in the world? They know they can always improve, and they show up in the off-season to shoot free throws when no one else is in the arena and hit the weight room like it's their part-time job . . . and nobody thinks they're broken. It's the same for the ambitious young account exec who gets an MBA or the tradesman who picks up new skills on the jobsite. Being better and reaching for that better version of themselves is not something to be ashamed of. It gets them to a place where they score more points, earn more money, stay employed longer, have status and respect.

So why don't the same rules apply when it comes to reaching for more internally? Working out a muscle in your arm doesn't imply you had bad arms before they were strong, but for some reason digging into why we do the things we do, how we're motivated, our habits, what we focus on—that work seems to call into question something at our core that defines us as either strong or weak, fit for more or destined for less, born with *it* or not. But can I let you all in on a little secret? All of us could benefit from reaching for more internally, from improving our mental health. All. Of. Us. Even you.

What I'd come to find out is that, no, self-help is not for broken people. I was struggling with brokenness but not broken. In fact, none of us is truly broken. We can suffer through seasons of hardship—we all have areas that are or have been fractured— but we are not broken in and of ourselves. If we know this bigger picture, we can admit the places where we are damaged and apply a salve to those wounds. And, once we get out of our distressed places, self-help is also for whole and healed people who want a fuller, richer life. It took admitting where I was damaged and applying that salve to see how it could help. That evidence revealed a huge gift: once I was out of my rut, I saw that the continued application of those tools can also take a healthy version of me further than I've ever been before, as a husband, as a father, as a man.

Now here's the thing: if you're already super into personal development—you're up early working on mindset, writing in a gratitude journal, listening to every growth podcast, searching for meaning with Viktor Frankl and all the rest—then none of this may be new. If that's you, I've got some even better books from more accomplished authors in the self-help space I'd like to refer you to in the back of this book. But if you've ever been skeptical of these tools or thought of those teachers as modern-day snake-oil salesmen who get rich by convincing insecure people to fork over their cash, I get you. I used to *be* you.

In part, I'm writing this for the person who isn't buying what they're selling, and I'm writing it because I was there just a moment ago. But for the last few years I've benefited from investing in and reaching for a better version of myself using the tools I once made fun of. I've changed my entire life—left my job, moved my family from Los Angeles to Austin, found my purpose, lived more fully into and up to the potential given to me by my Creator—and it wouldn't have happened if not for me saying yes to that one thing I swore I'd never say yes to.

I went to that personal-development conference.

About a week before the conference, I was out back with our boys attending to one of our nightly rituals called "ask any question," where our kids ask mostly disgusting questions that I promise to answer honestly. Nothing was off the table, but that night my middle son, Sawyer, who was seven at the time, asked an innocuous "What are you most afraid of?" He was fishing for tarantulas or scorpions, and out of my mouth fell, "Not living up to my potential." I teared up a little bit writing that sentence, and I don't even care if you judge me. I'd been living below my potential for such a long time, living into my very worst fear.

So, as Rachel and I took off for the conference, I had that conversation with the new loop running in my head. I had a mission. I was going to go to this stupid conference, and I was going to go all in. I was going to do it, jump up and down, drink the Kool-Aid, and figure out how in the world I could live up to this high bar of living into the potential I'd been given.

Yes, in the end, there were parts that were cheesy and, yes, I jumped up and down a lot and, yes, it was uncomfortable and, yes, *it absolutely changed my life*. There were plenty of things that weren't for me, but I have to give credit where credit is due—that conference fundamentally changed how I think about self-help. It offered tools that allowed me to better understand why I do and feel the things that I do, it shone a light on the lies I was believing that were holding me back, and it gave clarity on the roadmap I could follow if I wanted to take control of my life.

I came back on fire. The same kind of fire Rachel had come back with the first time around. I started getting up at 5:00 a.m. so I could get a jump start on my day, develop an exercise routine, and focus on some of my personal goals before the day began. I started thinking differently about what I wanted in my life, how I was going to get there, and whose permission I needed to chase after it. I started asking questions about where else I might find fuel like the fuel I'd just received and, in doing so, started a journey that would introduce me to other people focused on growth—authors and podcasts and couches that would change my thinking about what I could or couldn't be, how much was possible, and what societal constructs I needed to live inside, or, as it turned out for me, to live *outside*, to find fulfillment.

But the biggest thing I'm learning during my immersion in self-help is the tie between growth and fulfillment. You can find things short-term to make you happy, but if you want to truly be fulfilled you need to be growing. And in order to grow, you need to put in the time, do the work, and learn to kick the lies putting limits on who and what you can be.

In this book we'll deconstruct the lies that kept me stuck in the hopes it helps you avoid my mistakes. It's the same approach my wife, Rachel, used in her book *Girl, Wash Your Face*, though here it comes through the lens of a person not wired like her, with my motivationally challenged fixed-mindset leading to hyper pragmatism and an always-skeptical wiring. In the same way her book connected with readers who related with her stories, I hope my stories about fighting these lies might help you. In fact, we just debunked the first one here: the lie that *self-help is for broken people.*

Get Out of Your Own Way is a call to arms for anyone who's interested in a more fulfilled life, who, along the way, may have lost their "why" and now wonders how to unlock their potential or show up better for the ones they love. In doing the hard work of embracing growth and examining what lies I believed and why I believed them, I've become a better man for me, and for the relationships that mean the most to me in life. You can too. Make the choice to reach for more. The table is set. Now let's get to the lies we all need to stop believing to get there.

CHAPTER 1

THE LIE:
MY WORK IS WHO I AM

Ironically, the low point in my professional career was when I had the highest paying job and the most significant title I'd ever had. I was the head of sales at the Walt Disney Company's movie studio. In the simplest of terms, as president of distribution, I sold movies to theaters. I'd been doing this for seven years of a seventeen-year Disney career, and we were on a run. I don't mean we had some hit movies; I mean we had *all* the hit movies. We set every record. How could we not? I came into the job on the heels of the company's acquisition of Pixar, and not long after settling in we acquired Marvel Studios . . . and then LucasFilm.

In what will likely be regarded a hundred years from now as the beginning of the golden age for any movie studio ever, the collection of Disney's live-action films (like *Beauty and the*

1

Beast and *The Jungle Book*) and animated films (like *Frozen* and *Zootopia*), combined with the superhuman consistency from Pixar (*Toy Story 3, Inside Out*), the unprecedented Marvel run (roughly $10 billion in box-office earnings during my time), and the phenomenon of LucasFilm (all things Star Wars) came together to make box-office history. While I was distribution chief, we had the biggest year in the history of the business. And followed that with the second biggest year ever. We released nine of the ten most successful opening weekends ever. We had the biggest overseas numbers. We established our brands as the most prolific in entertainment and in doing so built something unlike anything the movie industry had seen up to that point.

I had the best team in the business, by a stretch. I was surrounded by the most incredible leadership team I'd ever worked with and was reporting to people whom I not only respected but who created an environment that people genuinely loved working in. Being involved with these epic brands also meant getting to collaborate with some of the greatest storytellers ever to work in this business. The talented actors who brought these roles to life? They were part of the mix too—going from people you dreamed of meeting one day to people you were picking up a past conversation with the next time you were at a premiere together.

All of it came with the romantic notions of Hollywood and the red carpets and the after parties. *And yet it was the low point of your professional career?* you may be asking.

Are you playing the world's smallest violin yet?

Do you need your head examined?

Well, yes, probably. But I can see clearly now that this lie that *my work is who I am* was keeping me from becoming who I was meant to be. How in the world is that possible?

It turns out that selling *The Avengers* and Star Wars to movie theaters isn't that hard. You don't need to fully understand the economics of how movie theaters work to appreciate that they need big movies to stay in business. So when you're the sales guy asking them to take your movie at a certain rate, there's a little less effort required than, say, my predecessor had to put in to sell *Wild Hogs*. Now, that's no dig on John Travolta, Martin Lawrence, and Tim Allen on dang motorcycles, and, yes, I'll watch anything where Ray Liotta is a bad guy, but the effort required to get a good deal for a movie about the midlife crisis version of *Sons of Anarchy* is wildly different than asking those same theaters to take *The Force Awakens*.

There was the crux of my unfulfillment. I was getting straight-A grades and didn't need to study. As the slate continued to grow and the teams hit their stride, turning out hits became more common and the fleeting effort required to make a sale left me feeling something that, for the longest time, I couldn't put my finger on. I got the biggest bonuses of my life, the most recognition of my career, and was the envy of others who had to work harder to do a similar job at other studios; and yet, because of that contrast, I was miserable.

I'm sure there's a part of you that wants to punch me in my miserable face. *What kind of high-class problems are you whining about, Dave?* I get it. But here's the thing: if you find yourself staying in the job you've had because it's become your identity or you're worried that pushing yourself into something that challenges you but requires shedding parts of that identity might not be received well by others, we've got plenty in common. I let the value others placed on my job or my title influence how I felt about myself, how present I was (or felt like I needed to be) at home, and, more importantly, how I pushed myself to fully use the potential I'd been given to show up for my life.

In my professional life I've been an assistant, coordinator, publicist, tour manager, producer, rep, director, varying levels of vice president, president, and now CEO. I have had all those titles over the twenty-five years I've been working, and even though they described the level of work I was doing, they didn't describe who I was. They didn't give me my value. At the time, I believed that they did, but believing it suggested that without the title, I was inherently less. That if I didn't have the right title or get promoted fast enough, I wasn't as good a person, or as able to contribute to society, or as capable of measuring up to the person I hoped to be.

Yes, I was proud of my ability to move from one level to the next, but in allowing my title and my worth in society to become so connected in my mind, I gave away my power to own my self-worth. This truth, this uncoupling of what I did professionally with who I am as a person, has created a long wished-for freedom from the worry of what other people think. And it has given me a forced focus on the reality I struggle to see or believe at times:

I can be a *good man* regardless of where I work, but where I work and what I do does not in and of itself make me a good man.

I can *provide for my family* in ways that make sense to me, but as I find ways professionally to provide, becoming more successful doesn't mean I'm justified in doing less at home as husband and father.

I can earn *respect* regardless of job title, and sometimes, it turns out, by abandoning that identity. It's on me, not my employer, to push me into places that help me *grow*.

I am *deserving of love* regardless of what my business card says.

I am *enough* before the commute begins.

But even when we hear or read truths like these, sometimes it is still hard to believe them and replace the lies we've held on to for so long. Why is that?

————

"When you think back to when you were a kid, which one of your parents did you crave love from most, and who did you have to be to get it?"

That was the welcome mat on the first day of that life-changing experience at my first personal-development conference. I'd never given it much thought. I'm sure most of us haven't. How we behave, both consciously and unconsciously, has roots that go back to our earliest memories as children and the kind of people we needed to be to get the reaction we were hoping for. The reaction most of us hope for is love, attention, affection, security, or some combination of these things, and the action we take to get it when we're five years old turns out to be the same one we use when we're ten and twenty and in the midst of a midlife crisis.

From my earliest memories, achievement was one of the things I associated with love. If I could collect the most trophies and lead the most social clubs and get selected for the honor society and make the sports teams and recite the Bible verses and get the good job, I'd get the pat on the back, the "we're proud of you" hug I craved. Those achievements were my road to love and, like so many others, I chased all the things to try and get it.

In hindsight, it's not like my parents really cared that much whether I got the best grades or had an extra sash on my graduation gown. But the reality I'd created in my mind, that achievement equaled love, drove so many of the decisions I made in every aspect of my life.

This pursuit of achievement drove me to jump from job to job inside the entertainment industry, each new job a new chance to show my parents and friends and peers that I was worthy of their notice. *Love me! Not because of who I am behind this job title but because of this job title.* Yep, it motivated me plenty, but, dang, is that an unhealthy way to go through life.

It's not like I knew it at the time. Heck, before I'd spent some time considering why I do what I do, it never really occurred to me to try to map out the things I had experienced in my life to better understand how those moments shaped me. Until I started digging into personal development and sat in therapy and did some work, I believed the illusion that I was in control of my actions. That's not to say that getting to a place where you're in more control isn't possible, but I came to realize that until you're able to better understand why you do the things you do, it's more likely that unconscious habits will kick in when life sneaks up around the corner and kicks you in the shin.

This lie that *my work is who I am* has shown up time and time again since my very first job. This book isn't long enough, nor the stories interesting enough, to go through them all, so instead let me give you three times during my journey at Disney when this phenomenon presented itself: once at the beginning, once in the middle, and once at the end.

THE BEGINNING

Early on at Disney I was placed into a job where I felt insecure about being the best fit. Only a couple of years in, I held a role where other candidates were more qualified, and I created a narrative in my head that everyone else in the organization was questioning my readiness and worthiness for the opportunity. I recognize now that I was projecting my own insecurities onto these people I was sure were judging me, but that's not what it felt like at the time. I worried constantly about being exposed as unqualified, and I had this crazy certainty that others were critical of my every move.

I knew logically that being insecure didn't serve me. That logic, though, was challenged by the ridiculous worry of a little boy from years earlier whose subconscious thoughts still found a way to voice lies. The name-calling from fourth grade wouldn't give way to the accomplishments of this grown adult. As much as you think it's you against the world, in these moments when you try to break away from the insecurities of your past, it truly ends up being you against yourself.

I was fortunate to have good coaches. The mistakes that came from listening to these voices of insecurity allowed those who cared for my development to shine a light into this area. That allowed me to be present in a way that was better for my teams, the bosses I was serving, and ultimately my personal brand. It was during this early *bigger-than-I-was-ready-for* job transition that a mentor dropped one of the best pieces of advice I've ever received.

Because I was worried that I'd be revealed as being in over my head at the time, whenever I found myself in a meeting and there was the slightest pause, I'd insert something that sounded smart (or at least sounded smart in my mind) so I could show the room how truly qualified I was for this role that I'd been given. Whatever that spark of brilliance was in that moment, it didn't necessarily have anything to do with my new role, or even the subject being discussed in the meeting, but, boy, did I think it was showing everyone how wrong they were to question my ability to do this new job.

After one particularly transparent showcase of my insecurities where I inserted every wise observation I could think of, my boss asked me to come to his office for a quick chat. As we walked down the hall, I wondered if I would get the traditional high five or if this could be one of those times we went all the way with a high ten. Was he going to give me a special certificate for my contributions that went above and beyond in a meeting? Would there be a statue unveiled of me delivering so much wisdom that we'd now memorialize that meeting for all time in bronze?

We walked into his office, the door closed, and he very calmly turned around and said four words that pierced my baby soul:

"Shut the f*ck up."

It was like the end of the *Mortal Kombat* video game I played as a kid.

Finish him. Fatality.

It was gutting. This person whose opinion I cared so much about and who I wanted so badly to think I was doing a good job just kneecapped me. He went on, "You are doing a great job. You are the best person for this role, and I wouldn't have put you there if that weren't the case. Stop worrying about what anyone thinks and prove what you can do with your results."

Oh. Okay. That sounds good.

It turns out, every time I opened my mouth in this attempt to prove my worthiness, I was taking a step in the opposite direction.

The advice served me well and was the beginning of a journey that had me taking new opportunities, making new mistakes, and finding, in a mentor, a mirror that could be held up to keep me accountable. Ultimately that would help me find better ways to stay out of my own way. I became more comfortable owning the spaces I didn't understand, yielded more and more to expertise when it appeared, and made a pivot from achievement being about my personal accomplishments to being about my ability to team-build and problem-solve by committee.

THE MIDDLE

Fast-forward a decade to when I was given the opportunity to run international theatrical distribution. It was a role far bigger than my résumé would have qualified me for, but it was a training ground that, in four or five years, could make me a candidate to take the role of head of global distribution. I grabbed my passport and got to work. But then, after only about nine months, due to a string of circumstances that could only be described as a mix of hard work, good timing, serendipity, and providence, I was thrust into the global head sales job.

The first three years were incredible, in large part because they were the most challenging. I walked into rooms where I was the least experienced person on an almost hourly basis and asked unbelievably dumb questions, did my best to listen, and was the beneficiary of the grace of teams who were willing to put up with my ignorance and teach me well. Some did it despite knowing that they would have been better candidates for my job. Most did it while stifling an eye roll.

Still, I had the job and the responsibility that came with it. In another layer of this lie of believing my work equaled my identity, I hoped my appointment to this role would affirm my inherent value and would, therefore, afford me the same kind of influence my predecessor had been afforded, a faith in my perspective, or at a minimum a willingness to give me the benefit of the doubt. I couldn't have been more wrong.

I got a preview of how hard those first few years would be when we needed to pick an opening weekend on the calendar for one of our upcoming movies. In the film business, talent of a certain caliber had contractual consultation rights for when their movies should come out, so in one of the final training-wheels moments before I assumed my new role, my predecessor, Chuck, had me lead his last meeting where we pitched Johnny Depp's team the rationale behind the date of his next blockbuster with us.

I studied all night and came ready to wow this assembled crowd with my knowledge of the calendar and the history of the movie business and the reasons this date on this weekend we'd picked would be better than any other date. I walked into the room and sat across from Johnny's lawyer and agent and manager and publicist and sister—the crew you had to convince. I knew them by reputation or photos on a red carpet but hadn't met them. Chuck, on the other hand, was embraced by each as they played a game of inside jokes and talks of the next time they'd golf together.

I slayed the meeting. I gave the most eloquent and compel-ling eight minutes of discourse on the reasons this date was the most perfect in all the land. I did it barely using notes and didn't need the help of my more experienced and familiar-to-them predecessor. I did all but land the plane with jazz hands, I was so proud of my articulate explanation. When I finished, I looked across the table and saw zero nonverbal cues. They looked like cyborgs. They did not smile or nod or stand up and applaud. They just sat there with blank stares on their faces.

After a dramatically long pause, the elder statesman in the room drew his gaze to my right and, in a deep, calm voice, said, "Chuck, what do you think?" Chuck smiled wryly under his classic mustache and said, "Well, in my business, this is a good date." And, to a person, the entire room in unison said, "Sounds good." The trust they'd built in Chuck over a couple decades of these meetings trumped every single part of my smooth delivery.

I was mortified. I was frustrated. What did this say about who I was if the people I was tasked with getting on board didn't see the authority of my position and therefore the value in me and my recommendations?

It said exactly what you think it did: *I hadn't earned their immediate nods.* It was an important hazing I needed to go through. It would take years of relationship building and exper-tise gathering before I got my version of "sounds good" from a room of people with contractual consultation rights. But this initial meeting humbled me and forced me to remember the fact that my job title did not equal my personal value, nor did it mean other people would automatically accept all my ideas.

In those early years in the role, I had to constantly remind myself that it wasn't a title or role that defined my ability to deliver value; it was my effort, my creativity in turning my inexperience into a *fresh-eyes* asset. Outside the office, my identity was not dependent on what work I did—to the people who really mattered, this was the least important consideration. Once I was able to clearly see these truths, I was able to come back with a healthier mindset and a fire in my belly to run faster and work harder, this time for the purpose of stewarding my job well rather than to feel better about myself or my worthiness in the role.

Those first three years as sales head were full of humbling learning experiences where my bosses and teams held my hand through teachable moments. I grew as the strength of the film slate grew, and, in what now feels like the blink of an eye, the drinking-from-a-fire-hydrant start turned into a drinking-from-a-water-fountain experience as I got the hang of things.

THE END

Being great at what you do is the goal, isn't it? In my last two years working at Disney, the records we were setting and the deals we were striking really were things to celebrate. I knew what I was doing, had the team and the films to fudge the rest, and got to a place where I was good at my job. Really good. Best-run-in-history, envy-of-the-industry kind of good. But the affirmation and adoration that was coming from the outside was so mismatched with the sense of dissatisfaction I was feeling on the inside. Why was I so much happier when the job was a struggle and so miserable when the going got good?

In the last two years of having the job of everyone else's dreams, I put responsibility for my unfulfillment on other people. It was Disney's fault for not giving me a bigger challenge, my boss's fault for not listening to my request for more responsibility, HR's fault for not advocating for me in new spaces with other business leads. It was my colleagues' fault for attempting to convince me that my feelings would be quieted in time, my industry's fault for assigning value to the role, my parents' fault for praising my accomplishments, my family's fault for needing the compensation that came from it. I couldn't grow because of other people. I couldn't leave because of other people. Other people.

I resented that *they* weren't doing more to fix my feelings.

Ridiculous. It took forever to realize that it was on me to fix this, to unwind this lie that kept my profession so integrally connected to my identity.

I am responsible for finding fulfillment in my job, for being happy with what I do, for knowing my value regardless of my title, the company I work for, the salary I make, or the way anyone looks at all of it. It took falling into a darker place to get the push I needed to address this more fully. I had to find the motivation to chase growth from within rather than relying on anything external.

It came down to intrinsic versus extrinsic motivation. I came to appreciate that you and you alone have to feel the call on your heart to grow and pursue a life that's better than the one you already have, even as it means shedding the identity you've become comfortable with in the office. If you can't let go of that identity you've allowed to become intertwined with your job in order to chase true happiness and fulfillment, if you don't take

13

responsibility for yourself and the significant steps needed to get there, you'll likely stay stuck. And it's not worth it. It's not worth it to cling to a false identity and sacrifice the *more* your life could be.

Pray for the wisdom to understand your potential, and for the strength, will, and drive to do the work required to bring those gifts to the world in a way that disconnects your job title from your ability to deliver impact. Though it took time and some bumpy roads along the way, this was the answer I'd been looking for. And once I was able to push past the fear and debunk the lies holding me back, it unlocked everything.

In what many saw as a crazy move, I quit. I left a great job full of security, opting out of a guaranteed multimillion-dollar annual salary and a position full of clout and prestige. I walked away to chase dreams with my wife. In a leap of faith, before her big book sold a single copy, we made the decision to move our family from LA to a small town just south of Austin, Texas.

Since making our move, I've grown more confident in who I am. And as much as my job is a component of who I am, I've found happiness in letting my actions as a supportive husband, involved father, and active ally for causes we believe in do the work in establishing my identity.

The truth that counters the lie that *I'm defined by my job*?

I am defined by my impact.

Impact is agnostic to job title. Impact can come irrespective of the name of your company. There's freedom in untangling what you do from who you are. Once you know your "why," you can find fulfillment in being challenged to chase it, no matter what your business card says.

THINGS THAT HELPED ME

1. **I redefined how I measured success in my work.** I'd been using a measuring stick that was more about what other people thought than how my potential was being used or how passionate I was about the work. But I shifted my focus to what really matters when it comes to work. Impact matters. Waking up on fire for the work matters. Feeling alive and whole while doing the work matters. Providing for your family can happen either way: in places where you aren't challenged or fueled and in places where it feels like a calling with maximum opportunity to use your gifts for others. Choosing to focus on the latter has made all the difference.

2. **I accepted responsibility for my career growth.** For too many years I sat stuck in a rut that I believed was caused by someone or something else. After having been the fortunate beneficiary of growth that I didn't have to drive myself, I didn't have the muscle memory to catalyze my own opportunities when things slowed. It wasn't until I took full responsibility for the work that only I could do to push myself that I started to see my skills tested in new, less comfortable ways that produced the growth I'd been missing.

3. **I worried first about my reputation as a human in the workplace.** When I felt myself descending because of the grip my career had on me and my identity, I made a conscious choice to advocate for others and be an ally. My voice as a leader of teams, the role I played as a mentor, the opportunities I chased with work-based philanthropy, or

my willingness to join a task force—all afforded a connection and value delivery that transformed how I felt about my work (as much as it had a nice side benefit of building my personal brand).

CHAPTER 2

THE LIE:

THE THINGS THAT HAVE WORKED ARE THE THINGS THAT WILL WORK

I was a great baseball player growing up. During T-ball and coach pitch, that is. I mean, I could really hit well when they placed the ball on a tee or grooved a nice slow pitch right down the middle. When they introduced live pitching from other small humans, though, my game took a step back. I was using the same approach for the at-bats from the previous season, and—surprise—it wasn't working.

So, I made adjustments, changed my stance, and moved up in the batter's box . . . and it worked. I recovered. I was great at playing baseball again. I had it down. These new things I knew would take me on to a long and prestigious professional career.

And then they started throwing curveballs.

While writing this book, I was in the early days of the biggest leap of my professional career. I'd spent two decades working in business environments that were big, or at the very least much bigger than the small-business arena I'm working in now. The situations that would come up in those big-business settings were the ones that had always come up, because those worlds were mostly about traversing trails that had already been traveled at different companies over and over since the beginning of time. Now I'm in this new role at a company that's less about trail management and more about trailblazing.

I left what I knew for what I needed.

I jumped into something foreign for the opportunity to be challenged, and the experience has been harder than I thought it might be. It's doing exactly what it's supposed to do in pushing me, but it's coming at the expense of my comfort. It's coming at the expense of my ability to control all the variables.

Of course it is. It's supposed to.

I'd been telling myself and anyone who would listen how important it is to push into new, unfamiliar work settings for the sake of growth. Over and over I'd been talking about the virtues of sitting in uncomfortable scenarios in order to be challenged by new and different sets of circumstances. Theoretically it made perfect sense. Once I actually embraced it, it *really* made sense. In that interim season, though, between theory and practice, I was taking the first steps toward situations where I could fail. I was living every day in an environment I wasn't familiar with and struggled to believe the things I was preaching. These were hard days where I worried more about being found out as unqualified than I believed benefit and growth would come out of this unknown.

As it turns out, this insecure feeling you get when you venture into new spaces, find yourself in new roles, or move away from what you know for what you need has a name: imposter syndrome. It's what happens in our brain that makes us doubt the things we've done, the qualifications we have—makes us worry we'll be discovered as a fraud.

Even though I had two decades of evidence to support my qualifications for taking on this new role in my wife's company, I struggled with the feelings of not having what it took to do the job since it was different from what I'd done previously. Despite all the things listed on my résumé, the organizations I'd led, the businesses I'd built, the way I'd been involved in things that would have suggested an abundance of competence for the job, I still found myself worrying that I'd be exposed as not having the specific set of expertise this unconventional job required.

I was walking into a company where revenues were driven by social media, publishing, digital education products, licensed merchandise and apparel, and live events. I have all this experience, but I've never worked specifically in *any* of these fields.

What's the lead time for manufacturing? What's a 3PL? The CRM platform? A "drip campaign"? What's the market norm for a licensing deal with a big-box retailer? The royalty rate for a book deal with one of the top five publishing houses? What kind of tech do we need to support live coaching? What is live coaching? What is tech? I walked in with so many questions.

I'd just left a job because it wasn't challenging enough, but my brain somehow twisted that. I found myself associating the successes of my past with serendipitous circumstances and, in doing so, stripped the impact that I, as an individual contributor, had on those successes.

I'd been incredibly successful doing what I *knew* for so long that I questioned my ability to do well when circumstances required me to learn and do new things.

Success can mess with you just as much as failure.

My deepest fears told me that my successes at Disney were a product of the brand, a result of the team surrounding me. Now that I was in an environment without the benefit of that name on the business card or the strength of those brands as part of my negotiating leverage, would I be shown to be a person who could only thrive when all the variables worked in my favor?

It was paralyzing. For the first six months, while I had a vision for where I wanted our business to go, it was always balanced against this anchor that held me back—a weight of insecurity that had me depending on muscle memory and what had worked for me in the past.

Things came to a head during the holidays. An unspoken frustration that had been brewing between me and my business partner (and best friend and wife) finally boiled over. She had been trying to give me time to figure it out, wanting to keep me happy, but my insecurities—and the subsequent clinging to what I knew from my previous work experience—were keeping our business from running optimally. So we had another in a series of hard conversations about what I really wanted in this role and whether the thing we'd been trying to do for the past half year was really the passion of my heart.

I was defensive. We'd built something that was generating the finances to support growing our team, impacting thousands and thousands of lives, and felt on the cusp of tipping into a mammoth enterprise whose influence would be felt around the world. I was so proud of what we'd built that hearing feedback was hard.

Two things were happening.

First, I was thinking that the things that got me here were the things that would get our company where we wanted it to go. I'd run businesses that lived inside of huge corporate environments for nearly twenty years. My last team had been composed of more than a thousand people from all around the world. My leadership style was one of empowering leaders to lead, where they'd come to me with issues and options for fixing them. I was used to flying at fifty thousand feet above the day-to-day operations. My people had been experts in their fields and often had more experience than I did, so I largely left them to do their thing while I managed the politics or stakeholders around the company or in the filmmaking community. I knew that operating style well. It had worked. But it was not an operating style that worked well for a small team in a start-up environment.

Second, I was secretly sitting in the fear that our newfound success with the Hollis Company was happening in spite of me, not because of me. I was worried that if I were to totally dig into the business, get fully invested in the details, be open to people asking for my perspective or pushing for more granular leadership, my lack of experience might actually work against this new team who, to a person, had more experience related to the job than I did—even if they didn't have experience doing specific tasks. Good times.

I clung to what I knew. With our small team, it meant most of our leaders were waiting to bring issues to me until they'd fully vetted solutions, and by the time they'd come to me, the problems had gone from easily solvable to *holy-cow-what's-going-on* kinds of issues. Even worse, because of the system I'd put into place, I wasn't aware of the issues holding us back.

We had massive learning bumps in launching our *Start Today Journal*, getting our documentary on Amazon, introducing live coaching to the community, building the back end for our podcasts, and installing the technology required to handle customer service needs.

All the things.

I can now so clearly see how these potholes and subsequent learnings made us stronger as a team, but at the time, they played against my biggest insecurities about being right for this job.

To make things worse, operating out of my old playbook meant I wasn't involved enough in the details to proactively navigate around potential bumps. I didn't know enough about what to watch out for, and I felt insecure in admitting it. As a result, we made less money, disappointed the community more than we should have, and had most of our team running too fast on a treadmill with no end in sight.

When it came to a head, I had the benefit of a business partner who was comfortable enough pushing the issue—even if it made things uncomfortable for a little while—to give us the opportunity to make it right. I had a founder and CCO who was willing, as she had been in the past, to come forward and risk it not being easy in order for it to be better. We'd had a conversation where she'd questioned my passion for being the CEO of the company. It stung. The next day Rachel sent me an e-mail that was a hard read and a totally necessary kick in the rear. She used one of her superpowers: making things crystal clear.

I know you are passionate about building this company. I KNOW that. What I asked was whether or not you're passionate about being CEO of a small business—it's very different than the job you had before. I worry, because you seem to be approaching it in the same way. You seem to be doing what you know instead of asking questions, trying to learn, and growing in the areas you aren't as strong. I admit my business weaknesses and failures all the time, because in that humility I'm able to learn and get help. It doesn't feel like you can receive negative feedback ever. Even last night, you never owned any fault; you only blamed the team for not telling you what's going on. Of course they should be more open than they have been, but even in that, the humble question would be, "How am I showing up as a leader in a way that makes my team afraid to come to me for help?"

You tell me I need to tell you what I want you to do—you've been saying that ever since we made the decision to join forces—but my frustration comes because I shouldn't have to tell you the problems we have at work. Don't you get that? Your team shouldn't have to tell you the problems. You should be so in the business that you KNOW our weaknesses and can work on the strategy to make us stronger. That's my frustration. You're not in the business; you're floating above it. A CEO can and should work from 50,000 feet—but not with a business, team, industry this new. Not when you've never done the work before. Maybe that's not what you believe but that's what I believe, and my frustration comes because I don't feel like I can tell the CEO of the company *I founded* things I'm concerned about.

You need to grow as a leader and do the work to learn how

managing a small start-up environment is different than what you've done before. It's not an indictment on your character or how awesome you are; it's just an area for improvement. Make a *standing appointment* to talk with the other CEOs + business heads you know. Listen to books on leadership: *Leaders Eat Last, Good to Great, 5 Dysfunctions of a Team, 21 Irrefutable Laws of Leadership* are some good ones. Find leadership or start-up podcasts, and absorb them daily. *Hope is not a strategy,* and right now you have no strategy to grow in this area. You love to tell the story about your old boss telling you to shut up in that meeting because it helped you grow. I know you don't like getting feedback from me, but I'm your business partner and this is my "shut up in the meeting" e-mail. You are massively talented—*and it's not going to be enough to get you where you want to be* or this company where we want it to go. We grow like warriors as fast as our business does, or we'll never turn it into what we know it can be.

I love you.

I know. It's magic. It felt like shit in the moment, but dang it, it did the job. These moments are the ones when my wife does the most important and hardest work in our relationship. Long ago we decided that having super honest conversations about our issues was more important than keeping each other feeling great about all things, but that doesn't take the sting out of hearing hard truths like this. Good news . . . I trust my wife and her instinct and the experience she's had with this community so much that, when she hits me with a two-by-four like she's Hacksaw Jim Duggan, I listen. Even when it hurts. Especially when it hurts.

So, out of a hard conversation came a change in approach. Just after receiving this e-mail I met with each of our team leaders and changed our operating model. We agreed as a team that I needed to ask more questions and roll up my sleeves and get my hands dirty rather than expect that everything would already be taken care of.

For me, it's been a process of unlearning two decades of a kind of leadership that made sense in one setting but didn't in this new one. It required that I put the worry of insecurity-fueled imposter syndrome to the side and do the damn work. This doesn't mean the experience from my past isn't valuable. Of course it is. It simply means that the experiences from my past have to be put to use in a different kind of way. The things that got me here will not be the things that get me, our marriage, our kids, or our company where we need to go.

THINGS THAT HELPED ME

1. **I had to roll up my sleeves and do the work.** Rachel knows how to do the job of every single employee at the Hollis Company. She knows it, because in building it for the past fifteen years, she's had to do every single job at one time or another. I do not yet know how to do every single job, but I've committed to learning. What are the "jobs" in your relationships, your household, and your place of work that you don't yet know how to do but need to? In a world that moves as quickly as the one we're living in, leaning on how you were raised or what you learned in school may very well make you obsolete

if you're not willing to roll up your sleeves and do the work.

2. **I asked every single possible question.** There can be stigma against asking questions. If you ask a question about something you don't know, does it reveal you to be a person who doesn't know everything? You bet. So you have to choose, like I did, whether you want to be revealed as a person who doesn't know everything in the attempt to know more, or if you want to be ignorant and full of pride. You may convince yourself that your pride is worth not knowing as much, but you won't go as far or have nearly the impact as the person who's informed. Rachel models this for me every single day.

3. **I let my inexperience act as an opportunity instead of a liability.** In any new environment, the willingness of an experienced operator to listen, learn, and then ask questions about pieces of the process can be a massive strength. Rather than seeing my lack of experience as a barrier, I turned it around and asked whether my objectivity from having not been in the day-to-day of the operation could bring up angles that hadn't yet occurred to the folks who had been in it for longer, and who had become too close to it. It's like seeing the forest rather than the trees. In most cases, the blend of new eyes and old hands have produced extraordinary results.

CHAPTER 3

THE LIE:

I HAVE TO HAVE IT ALL TOGETHER

Be it at 20th Century Fox, the talent agency BNC, Merv Griffin Enterprises, or Disney, I have negotiated business deals for the better part of twenty-five years. These deals involved the biggest names and brands in entertainment, generated billions of dollars in profit, and the incremental benefit from these transactions improved the economics on "our side" by ten-digit swings. Big deals. Lots of negotiations.

When I first started, I was clumsy. I approached things with brute force and adversarial confrontation, which set a tone that didn't always make things go as well as they should. I believed I needed to show unwavering strength at all times to get the outcome I was looking for. I believed I had to put on a facade of "having it all together" so I wouldn't somehow compromise my negotiating position. Every single time, I'd go in combatively and the other side would come back at me with the list of reasons why my strong position wasn't reasonable, tenable, or appropriate. It created a gulf we had to cross to reach a deal and usually strained the relationship, requiring way more work, so much more emotion, and often resulted in poorer deals.

Then I watched *8 Mile*. Yes, the movie about Eminem as B-Rabbit, a white rapper in Detroit trying to make his way out on the back of winning rap battles. That *8 Mile*. The end of the movie features an underground tournament championship pitting Eminem against Anthony Mackie (yes, Falcon was a rapper first). Eminem led with everything negative that could be said about him in this battle: he was white, he lived in a trailer with his mom, he'd gotten jumped before, and his girlfriend was unfaithful (it's unbelievably more graphic, but you get the picture). He didn't put up a front. But, in admitting everything that his rap battler could possibly use against him, by embracing confidently that he absolutely did not have it all together, he took all the power away from his opponent. So much so, spoiler alert, that Mackie didn't even try to come back with a rap after this devastating performance.

It turns out inspiration really can come from anywhere. Who in the world would have guessed that Eminem would have a serious impact on my negotiating style at work? I started every negotiation differently from that point on. I thought about what they would come at me with, which of my position's weak points they'd attack, and I brought them up *before* they did, addressing them honestly and cutting off the possibility that they could exploit those weaknesses or surprise me with them.

Someone's going to take a swipe at me for being the new guy? *I am new to this business, but that fresh perspective may allow me to see things others aren't looking for.*

Complaints that this is the way business has always been done? *Uber is the biggest brand in transportation and doesn't own cars. Airbnb is the biggest name in hospitality and doesn't own property. Doing things differently is the way to innovate and grow.*

They're telling me nobody has to pay rates this high? *I understand that these are the prices you've traditionally paid, but this personality/product/brand isn't traditional either. You don't take percentages to the bank; you take absolute dollars. We'll have you covered there.*

When I first acknowledged what could be seen as weaknesses, addressing them before pivoting to what we needed from the deal, the other side was left with fewer moves. Part of this was because of the surprise of hearing so transparently from us, but part of it was because we'd inoculated ourselves from the most powerful barbs they'd have thrown at us if we hadn't already deconstructed them ourselves.

It worked well.

It worked so well that I began to ask better questions about where else negotiations were happening in my life. And then I was struck with an epiphany: Every interaction we have is a negotiation of sorts. Every conversation with our partner, the way we hope to motivate our children, the attempts to connect in friendships, all of them are a kind of negotiation. Was there a chance that if I employed some of the same tactics that had worked in my professional life it might bear fruit in my personal life as well? Were there things I was missing out on personally because of this posture I'd been keeping up of having to have everything together?

Of course there were.

Once I started owning the areas where I wasn't feeling confident with Rachel, where I was struggling with my closest friends, and even being more honest with my kids about how a grown-up processes feelings, it created an empathy and connection of shared experience. No one has it all together, and the people who are willing to admit that freely, who are willing to admit that first, will disarm and connect with the people they care most about in life. There are so many things we all universally struggle with, and when someone acknowledges this, we can't help but be drawn to them.

It can be lonely, isolating, and hard to find people to come alongside you if you don't own your struggles. If you're basing relationships on a front of *everything being okay*, are you really building an authentic relationship? As someone who for too long believed that representing strength was the way, I can tell you with certainty that it was only when I began connecting with people as my authentic, everything-not-all-together self that I was able to form relationships that were deeper, more meaningful, and available to support me in the seasons I needed them most.

When I was most stuck, *my willingness to raise my hand and acknowledge I needed help was the reason I was able to get help*—and it was only in getting help that I was able to get out of my mess.

The notion of *disruption* is one of the single greatest ingredients in innovation today. In a world where wearing masks of perfection and inauthentically assuring the masses that all is good, the person who's willing to own their imperfections and deviate from the cultural norm will embody disruption in a way that creates for them an unfair advantage in their life, their work, and their relationships. Be that kind of disrupter.

THINGS THAT HELPED ME

1. **I used vulnerability as a strength.** Whether you're in a business or personal relationship, being open about the things you're struggling with makes you relatable, allowing you to connect more authentically. Whatever taboo you associate with admitting the things that aren't great about your life, once you flip that narrative in your head, you'll open yourself up to the possibility of community and results on a whole different level. Added bonus: if you're in need of help, when you exhibit a little more honesty and vulnerability, you'll actually have a shot at receiving what you need.

2. **I preemptively acknowledged my weaknesses.** In your personal relationships, when you get ahead of your weaknesses and are able to be honest in owning your experience, not only do you create a bridge of empathy with the ones you're trying to connect with, you can also manage the narrative around why those weaknesses exist and how they could be overcome. Your insights will humanize you and may even be a tool that someone else in your life can use to overcome a similar challenge. Talking openly about the things I've struggled with has proven to be a bonding agent in my relationships.

3. **I learned to give an honest representation of myself from the start.** Too much of our time is spent trying to parse through what's real and what's not, what matters and what doesn't. If we start our conversations from a place that's more honest, authentic, and real, the chances that we'll get to a deal, a meaningful relationship, the help we need when we need it, or achieve a desired goal are remarkably higher. Waste time with games, or get there quicker with a more honest representation of who you are and where you're at.

CHAPTER 4

THE LIE:

A DRINK WILL MAKE THIS BETTER

Speaking of *having it all together*, this may be the chapter where you ask for a refund. If you were hoping you were reading a book from someone who has it all figured out and is running without bumps along the way, my friend, this is where I spoil the ending. A "Bruce Willis is dead the whole time" kind of spoiler.

I've been in a constant battle with my vices over the last three years. I'm talking about the behaviors you know you shouldn't do but find yourself doing anyway. I'm talking about having the vision of yourself where you are your very best . . . and acting in the total and complete opposite way. I have experience in this.

Vices were there to soften the sharp edges in a season when I wasn't growing.

When I tripped my way through the midlife bridge.

When I left the corporate identity that made sense to everyone else.

As I got oriented in this new, unconventional job.

Even as I embarked on the ambition of writing this very book.

In this recent stretch, I turned leaning on my vices into a survival habit. A habit I didn't really give much thought to, and one that definitely didn't serve me or the growth I was hoping might come.

It turns out writing a book has been something of a trigger for me. Every one of these chapters, in a strange way, has required an introspection and honesty that usually only shows up in therapy. On the comfortable couch of someone named Debra (I've changed the spelling of her name from its traditional Deborah to protect her identity), it's super easy to talk about all the things you feel shame over. Or easier at least. It's a totally different thing to own what you feel when you know that other humans will read it, and that difference has made it hard for me to control some of the bad habits I've turned to over time to mute the stuff I don't like to think about.

My vices exist to quiet the things I don't want to deal with.

Unfortunately, though, in my experience, coping that shows up as a negative character trait often leads us to believe we are, in fact, negative ourselves. A vice that shows our defects can make us believe we are defective. That creates a nasty circle and makes it feel even harder to keep on the path toward growth.

Listen: I know growth happens outside our comfort zones and is the only way to fulfillment—I know these things to be absolute truths—and yet I'm in the midst of my full submersion in this pursuit and can tell you, it's hard. It's hard to sit in places that you don't know; it's hard to try things you haven't tried before. It's hard to grow.

I know it's supposed to be hard, but I'm learning in real time the trade-off between the healthy and unhealthy ways of handling hard things. I've taken the unhealthy path more often than I'd like to admit, and here I am telling you that, in chasing all the things that will help me grow, I have to work harder now than ever to stay out of my own way. You'll have to work harder than ever as well.

The transition in my life over the last few years has been wildly successful, and violently disruptive to my sense of normalcy. I feel vindicated by the results, and consistently insecure about what this new normal is supposed to feel like. Growing into who we've been called to be is inspiring . . . and freaking scary.

For me, I've tended to turn to alcohol. Yes, over the years I've struggled with smoking cigarettes, and online poker, and too many video games, and gambling on sports, and working out like a crazy person, and on and on . . . because I'm an overachiever and usually go big or go home. But if we're going to be really honest, I tend to turn to alcohol to numb my worry when stuff feels like it's out of my hands, to unconsciously self-sabotage when I feel insecure, even to manufacture stakes when things in my life got easy.

Drinking was a lonely, shameful part of my life. I drank alone. I drank more than anyone knew. I drank vodka so people couldn't smell it on my breath. I drank just about every day, just a little more than I should, for far too long. I hit points where Rachel could see it in a quick stumble at the end of a night. I felt the embarrassment of a hangover in the drop-off line at school in the morning.

It anchored my mood to the floor.

It crushed my motivation.

It affected our sex life . . . yes, it messed with *the thing* you're thinking.

I'd convinced myself that a drink would make things better, but the only thing it did was kick the can on down the road, taking parts of my life that kept me getting in my way and making them worse for not dealing with them head-on.

My entire life I've stayed tethered to a belief that a higher power is pulling the strings here and, in doing so, is complicit in opening doors—including the doors that provoke my anxiety, the doors that trigger my insecurity, the doors that, in seasons of feeling unfulfilled, have had me subconsciously self-sabotaging to create challenges. I know intellectually that life is happening for me, that these things are happening to pull out a greater version of myself, but then somewhere in my unconscious, where my deepest insecurities live, that rational argument frays.

I used to cling to the idea of having a sense of control over what happens next. But I've come to appreciate that *feeling like I'm in control isn't actually part of the plan.*

A life of growth means a life of exhilarating discomfort. That's the actual plan, and as a result, the last few years produced a season of "control" challenges. As in, there is no controlling this new constant that is the chaos of our life. As in, in the times when I feel I have less control over life, I tend to believe I also have less control over how I deal with that loss of control.

When things got crazy, I alleviated crazy with a drink. Or four drinks. Don't judge me. Well, actually, go ahead and judge me. I had to. So did Rachel. I had to judge what good it was doing for me to try and mute my feelings rather than deal with them.

I had to judge if this alcohol plan was sustainable long-term (it isn't) or if it served me at all (it doesn't). I had to judge if there was more good in digging into what was triggering my reaction than trying to not deal with it.

If you want a meaningful life, you must create situations that make you uncomfortable.

Comfort is a casualty of growth.

If you aren't willing to put your comfort at risk, you'd better prepare yourself to settle for a mediocre life. I don't want mediocre. You don't either. If we're going to chase more, it's going to come with the reality that we'll have to risk more. We're going to have to risk our usual, safe, normal lives. It's going to feel uncomfortable—because that's where the growth comes from.

Muting discomfort doesn't feed growth; it stifles it. I get that now.

When medicating my anxiety during our transition from California to Texas turned into me drinking a little too much a little more often, Rachel confronted me in a way that only she could:

You want to get anxiety under control? Do the work. You want to drink less? Take it seriously. Get a plan. Stop before you have too much.

I've been trying to help you with these problems for two years, and I'm tired. Stop talking about it and start doing something about it. You are in control of your life. Your shame doesn't serve you when you make a mistake! Do the work, get the help if you need it, and stop making excuses.

I love you, Dave, but I can't save you. You need to save yourself.

Tough love . . . for the second time in four chapters. I know. A guy can react to this in one of two ways: grab another drink and drown away the challenge from a woman who loves you, or sit in a posture of gratitude for the willingness of a partner to push you to step up for your life. On the first day I read this note, I felt more like the former, but every day since, I've been living in the latter. It's hard to have a mirror held up to your face. Hard to deal with the ridiculous things we do when we let our unconscious minds make bad choices for our lives. It's not fun to be called on the carpet, but it's necessary.

Some of you may not be married to a woman as strong, confident, and crazy as Rachel Hollis. Let me channel her for those of you who need to hear this: *You need to save yourself.*

Whatever your vice, your coping mechanisms, the set of habits that don't serve you or the ones you love, it's on you. It will be hard and take work, but it starts with *you choosing* to do the work and take control.

Of course, some of you may not like the idea of having to hold yourself accountable, may not like what you see when you're forced to take a serious look in the mirror. I didn't. But being forced to do it was a gift afforded to me by someone who thought more of me than I did myself during that season. I was challenged to believe in myself as much as she believed in me.

I'd negotiated with myself plenty. There were more than a few *I've had a hard day—I deserve these drinks* thought bubbles to help me rationalize pouring another. But with the gauntlet thrown, I had to ask if I needed the drinks more than my kids needed an intentionally present dad. If the benefits of numbing my anxiety took precedence over being the exceptional husband I vowed to be for my wife. If taking the edge off a long day came at the expense of building a business and responsibly supporting a growing team.

I *earned* that drink, but they deserved better.

As important as a good dose of accountability and perspective was in coming to fully appreciate the truth about coping mechanisms that numb—you can't numb the pain without numbing the joy. It is impossible to close off your anxiety without also eliminating the growth that comes from fully experiencing discomfort. In this pursuit for fulfillment, I reached for a muting agent to handle the unsteadiness of the new waters I was in. Only after diving into these hard conversations could I see that so long as I tried to mute the disruption of the waves, I would not experience fulfillment. Those waves, they weren't an obstacle; those waves were the means to the end I'd been so desperately looking for.

John Maxwell once said, "Most successful people will point to the hard times in their lives as key points in their journey of development. If you are dedicated to growth, then you must become committed to managing your bad experiences well."[1]

I don't want to discount the disease that is addiction in any way. If you are someone who truly can't control your impulses and are making choices that don't serve you, your relationship, or your future, own it. Get some help. Quit letting pride be the barrier between you and a version of you that can more aptly handle the crap you're dealing with. For far too long, I didn't want to really acknowledge the choices I was making (or the choices I was subconsciously making to not have to actually deal with my stuff). Once I was able to ask better questions while being honest about how I was coping, I could deal with my insecurities and fears in a way that served me.

When I sat and really thought about how I wanted my life to look, both how I am present in relationships and the ambitious plans we had for growing our team, I knew I had to take serious action.

I committed to staying present in the chaos and friction of these big moves and new learning curves. As my friend Brendon Burchard would say, I decided to "honor the struggle." I had to be honest about the triggers that might lie ahead as we scaled our business. I had to ask, what would it mean to show myself that I don't need a drink? Or that not having one might afford me the opportunity to actually receive the benefits?

In real time, I haven't had a drink in more than five months. In doing so, I have been more focused as the complexities of the business have scaled. I have been more productive as the team has grown from four to forty-four in the past year, all while writing this book. I've been more engaged with my kids and more intentional with my wife. I've dropped weight and have more energy and a sex life that's better than ever. Bless up. Literally.

Most importantly, I've shown myself that I don't need alcohol to deal with anxiety and stress. I've rewired the way I think about the necessity of a drink on a long flight, or as an accomplice on vacation or the requirement for fun. I've shown myself I can do a thing that seemed impossible five months ago after twenty-five years of casual drinking gave way to something more than casual.

Now that I know I can do the impossible, I believe I can do anything.

When this book hits shelves, I will not have had a drink in 338 days. I committed to a year of sobriety the day the edits came back on the words you're reading—trust me, a trigger if there ever was one.

As reinforcements for Dave 2.0, I added a healthy eating plan, put together a gym in our garage, and committed to workouts or running every single day. I talked openly with friends, family, and mentors about my decision to intentionally pursue healthier choices. I reconnected with my therapist to leave a line open as needed. I went all-in on a complete reboot of mental and physical health, and the introduction of a new set of habits have had a remarkable effect.

The mindset change of embracing the necessity of discomfort for growth has been a springboard in this season. It led to climbing 29,029 vertical feet in a weekend. It had me finish my first marathon. It has me on a perpetual, intentional pursuit of hard things. You see, the *need* to numb drastically reduces when you actually believe growth is supposed to be uncomfortable.

If I had been willing to sit with the heavier consequences of these new things I was being challenged with, it would have forced me to grow into a bigger, more resilient, and stronger version of myself than the one who chooses booze or anything else to mute the tension. Now that I see that the struggle, the resistance, is *the way*, I know that the idea of muting it with a vice is totally and completely counterproductive. I choose instead to lean in and feel it fully, even though it's hard.

For you it may not be alcohol, but we all have a coping mechanism that, if we leave it unattended, can spin into something that gets in our way. If you're stuck behind a lie that has you using food, drugs, sex, sleep, passive aggression, self-harm, bad hygiene, withdrawal, or anything else to keep you from processing the thing you *need* to feel to grow, choose discomfort over coping. Choose growth over the unhealthy things that are going to keep you in your own way.

It won't be easy.

It will be worth it.

THINGS THAT HELPED ME

1. **I got to the root of why I turned to vices.** The idea that a drink could make my stresses better was built on a foundation of believing that the drink was a better option than anything else I might interject to take the drink's place. Now that I see how the cocktail was an answer to a question of how to calm nerves, I've learned to ask myself what better answers might exist. I've substituted those—working out, sitting in therapy, talking with a mentor, being honest with my business partner/wife—for the impulse to drink and mute.

2. **I kept coming back to the devastating impact of muting life in an attempt to avoid a single thing.** The notion of drinking (or, insert your vice here) to help you mute your anxiety or frustration or fear presupposes that you can use it as an accurate local anesthetic rather than a general pain suppressant. The more time I've spent understanding the impact of my vices, the more I appreciate that the muting of the bad also comes with the unwanted muting of all the good. Making choices that could minimize the good just to control the bad isn't going to bring out the best in my life, so I won't walk down that road.

3. **I committed to a team of accountability partners for the areas where I struggle.** I'm a good dude, and I can't do this alone. At a recent lunch with three of my buddies, I had to give it to them straight: that I was leaning on alcohol to calm my anxiety and that, if I was going to get through it, I would need them to support me when we were hanging out, to check in with me on the regular, and to encourage me to drink the crap out of my sparkling water. I also sat with my wife, and we committed to being a team in this. This problem has become our problem that we'll solve together. Don't think you have to get through your struggles with vices alone. Rather, stack the odds in your favor to train yourself to make choices that serve you, supported by the people in your life who can help you get where you're hoping to go.

CHAPTER 5

THE LIE:

I DID SOMETHING WRONG, SO I AM SOMETHING WRONG

I was valedictorian at my high school, set to give the commencement address on the greatest day of my life to that point. I had a special white robe in a sea of black that paired well with a blue sash for an honor society, some medals of some kind, and gold braided ropes that hung around my neck for an achievement I can't remember. I basically looked like one of those military leaders from a dictatorship and walked around with an air of confidence like that of a conquering general.

Four years of hard work, built on top of the eight that preceded it, would all be on display that day. My parents, grandparents, extended family, and friends would all be witness to

my awesomeness. It was going to be epic. I mean, it would have
been epic.

I didn't end up getting to walk at graduation.

Or give my commencement speech.

I got suspended on the last day of high school.

Like Donna Martin from West Beverly High.

For being a jackass.

If you know me at all, you know I'm a joker. My sense of
humor has been part of me for as long as I've been alive, and it
was part of my persona through high school. My ability to make
people laugh was an awesome asset during an awkward phase
of life, but it was also what gave administrators pause as they
considered giving me the podium on the last day of school. I'd
taken some liberties as an emcee of assemblies that veered off
script in the past and, while they were hilarious (if I do say so
myself), this made them wary, as the important final-day ceremony needed to be handled seriously.

I was committed to doing it right, to delivering an address
that would show I could be the professional they needed on
stage when it was called for. I gave up my lunches for a month
to spend time with a speech coach (while my peers were living
their best end-of-school lives), working over and over on my
pace, delivery, and how to put emphasis on the words I wanted
to land best. I'd heard administrators' concerns over and over,
had told them at one point that if they didn't have confidence
in me as the choice for speaker they should swap me out, and
was now doing my best to stay focused.

The day of graduation I was all nerves. At the run-through
that morning, we blocked out the steps for what would be
an afternoon show, and I sat in that front row head down,

rereading a script I'd been through a thousand times. I was in a zone.

And then it happened.

It startled me when the principal walked up and took the script from my hands. He said, "You will read this, and only this," and my nervous, exhausted-from-the-questioning self broke a little. When he dropped the script on the grass at my feet, I snapped.

As he walked away, I gave him the old one-finger salute. I did it in an impulsive, emotional moment, and once it was seen by another staffer, the old snowball started rolling downhill. I lost my mind. Used every word in the book. I used curse words I didn't even know existed. I directed them at the principal and basically anyone who was older than eighteen years old on-site. It was an out-of-body experience. It was the greatest day of my life, until it wasn't.

Instead of driving to graduation with my parents later that day, I got to meet them at the school office hours before the ceremony started. In an interruption of the decorating and dip making that was happening at the house, they got to come watch a piece of paper slide across a desk, letting me know that I was officially suspended and not allowed to be on school property for the rest of the day.

I was devastated.

My parents were devastated.

My grandparents and extended family who were starting to arrive at the house for a graduation party were all grappling with the rug pull.

Sure, there were a bunch of things I think the school could have done differently in the events of the day—and it took me years to actually see this objectively—but I understand now that I really *did something wrong*. In a moment when I had a choice to make, I chose not to respect authority or follow the rules and acted like a total jackass. I didn't deserve to give my speech. I deserved to be suspended.

For months, in the aftermath of that very bad day, these events were the last thing I thought about before I fell asleep and the first thing I thought about when I woke up. I was convinced it would be that way for the rest of my life. *How dramatic.*

More than that, in having let down the people who meant the most to me in my life, including myself, because I did something wrong, I thought it *made me something wrong*. In fact, it's an idea that Brené Brown addressed in a fantastic TED talk where she gets into the distinction between guilt (*"I did something bad"*) and shame (*"I am something bad"*). I can relate.[1]

I carried that lie around like a weight for a very long time. Seems silly now, when you think about what happened relative to everything else life could and has thrown my way, but it's a thought I've had to battle through every time I've made mistakes since then in my adult life.

Doing something wrong doesn't make you wrong at your core; it makes you human. I say this as a good man who has tried his best and who has done some really stupid stuff in his life. I say this as a guy who just spent a chapter talking about slaying a drinking dragon, who regularly makes mistakes as a dad, who's learning to become a better leader every time I stumble.

This isn't going to be the longest chapter, because it doesn't need to be. In as simple a way as I can say this: you are good and enough just as you are, flaws and all. I can hold that notion of you being fundamentally good and enough as you are today and simultaneously hope that you will learn from your humanity to become something more. The learning you can take from those missteps that didn't serve you or your relationships? Those learnings will light the way for where you need to go. Learning from those times when you were wrong is what ultimately builds character.

We are the result of the life we've lived, but we only become prisoners of our mistakes if we allow it. You get to write the story of how your flaws have made you stronger today. You get to decide how you'll use the narrative of what's happened to you to create what happens to you next.

Choosing to learn from your mistakes, ask for forgiveness, express contrition, and go to therapy as needed to process these wrongs—those are steps in the learning process that can take your experience and turn bad to good. Staying wrapped in an identity as someone who's wrong, who's broken, who's not the kind of guy or gal who deserves certain things because of choices in your past? That's allowing those decisions to imprison you, letting a person you no longer are condemn you to a life that's less than what's available to you.

The sooner you can shift the way your mind interprets the indiscretions of the past—from a lifetime indictment of you as a person to a lapse in judgment that you can learn from—the sooner you can apply the lessons to achieving your goals. Some of the biggest mistakes I've made in my life have become cautionary tales that now inform how I love my wife, how I lead my team, how I parent my kids. Many of them have shown themselves in retrospect to have been the vehicle for some great breakthroughs, setting me up for success by providing a map for how not to navigate what's in front of me next time.

For some of us, our identity and significance have become anchored to our past failures as we allow these things to define us and, in doing so, create limitations for what we consider possible. This becomes the narrative we believe, and we hold tight to the excuses that narrative affords us because of how comfortable we've become in identifying that way.

Let go of that identity.

Let go of those excuses.

Good people do dumb things. Dumb people are the ones who don't find a way to learn from those things. I've learned a ton from graduation day and every mistake I've made since. Don't be dumb.

THINGS THAT HELPED ME

1. **I countered shame with sharing.** We all suffer from things we are ashamed of, having done things we know we should not have done. Holding on to that shame, drowning in that shame, letting that shame become part of our identity—that does not serve us in any way. The antidote to shame? Empathy. Brené Brown said, "Shame depends on me buying into the belief that I'm alone,"[2] and she encouraged finding someone you can share this shame with so that, in the expression of empathy, you might wipe out that emotion. When I've struggled, finding someone to work through my struggle with has helped me evict the shame I've carried.

2. **I found examples of others who struggled and learned from how they turned their pain into power.** When

you're going through a hard time, it's easy to feel like you and you alone are dealing with these hard circumstances, and even easier to feel like these choices are happening *to you* rather than *for you*. What if you saw a model of someone else who made the same set of bad decisions but learned from their journey and came to a stronger place on the other side? When I was able to see how universal and common my struggles were by reading books and listening to podcasts from people who'd gone through similar seasons, it changed the way I thought about the possibilities of what might come from my mistakes . . . in a good way. I'm the strongest I've been because of the mistakes I've made, and I'll tell my story to as many as I can in the hopes that it will help someone who sees themselves in it to change the narrative of what's possible in their life too.

3. **I changed the way I thought about asking for help.** In a strange way, some aspects of masculinity made me think even needing help was an indication of weakness. If I couldn't do something on my own, fix it myself, take care of my own issues, what kind of a man was I anyway? The reality is, I'd been taking help from people all the time and never once felt like it undercut my manhood: letting a doctor or contractor or chef or one of a number of experts do their thing in my life. When I thought differently about what it might mean to reach out to and use the expertise of people who could help me with my mental health, overcome the mistakes I'd made, understand why I do the things I do, I was better for having put myself in their qualified hands—and maybe more a man for having allowed it to happen rather than trying to fix it on my own.

CHAPTER 6

THE LIE:

EVERYONE IS THINKING ABOUT WHAT I'M DOING

I was a nerd growing up. I mean, I'm a nerd now, but I like that part of me in a way I didn't embrace as a middle schooler. Middle school sucks for a nerd. When you're trying to survive middle school as a bizarrely tall, freakishly skinny, acne-strong honor-roll student, fitting in and finding a crew is a must. So I reached for Sea Scouts.

Genius.

In my backward, ridiculous, newly teen mind, joining a co-ed version of Boy Scouts with boats felt like the right choice. Not only could this up my game socially, but I reasoned that it might even help me get a human of the opposite sex to take notice of me. I took the classes and got the gear and found my way out on the seas, hoping to impress my first crush, this likely future wife.

I did all the things I thought might impress her. Learned the knots and the terminology and had the uniform and passed the safety tests. I was going to be the best scout, because of course the girl always falls for the best scout.

The dry-land part went so well. When we graduated to actual boats, though, I found the flaw in my logic.

Motion. Ocean.

I had done all the work and played all the cards right, but when it was time to close the deal and seal this thing long-term, I barfed. I mean, I threw up everywhere. I was mortified. What would she think? How could we possibly get married now that she knew I was this lame? How could I possibly salvage this budding romance?

The next day, I made my way up to her to try and explain myself. As I stood in front of her, sheepishly looking for some sign that I hadn't blown my chance, she gave it to me straight:

"What's your name again?"

Ouch.

Here's a gift that will serve you even if you're not a middle school boy looking for love: nobody is thinking about you.

They're thinking about themselves.

Shelly wasn't thinking about me and what I'd done that day on the boat (I'm guessing she was preoccupied with whether she herself was going to puke). And most people you do life with every day aren't thinking about you either.

That's not an indictment of the people in your life; it's just a truth about the human condition. We are all worried about ourselves, and any reaction we have to other people tends to be a reflection of our own insecurities. *If someone does have a problem with something you're doing, it's likely they are challenged by it, feel insecure because of it, are jealous of your willingness to chase after it, or are frustrated that your belief in yourself makes them more aware of their disbelief in their own ability.* In the end, it's rarely actually about you.

This isn't to say that some folks don't have legitimate concerns about the choices you're making and whether those choices fuel you. You know when people's motives are pure and in your best interests. You should listen to those people. They're that small percentage who really knows you and your heart, the desires and motives of your soul. Rather, I'm talking about the collective "they" and the worry of letting them down that tends to keep us inside our comfort zones, and keeps us from reaching for more.

In my career I've moved from six different entertainment companies where I held seventeen various jobs over twenty-five years. Every time I knew it was time to leave a post, the biggest barrier to my leaving was the worry of what other people would think. In each instance I was walking away from something that those living in the world I was departing had assigned significant value. In the most recent transition from distribution president to start-up CEO, I was moving away from something that made so much sense to the traditional entertainment industry to pursue something that didn't play by their rules. The idea that what was better for me could exist outside of what "they" had given value to and committed their lives to was going to be hard for them to appreciate and hard for me to challenge. I was sure of it.

I barely slept in the weeks leading up to the reveal. I worried people wouldn't get it. And if they didn't get it, I would start second-guessing myself. At a minimum I was sure people would be confused. No matter what, they'd be disappointed.

It was just after the turn of the new year in 2018. After a week of sleeplessness, I told my bosses, my team, creatives at the studios, partners at talent agencies, and the press about my plans to leave the greatest media company on earth (Disney) for the second greatest media company on earth (the Hollis Company).

As it turned out, none of my fears actually played out the way they had in my head. Well, some of them may have been realized (most people definitely didn't get it), but my worry about their effect was wildly out of proportion.

My bosses were unbelievably generous in their response. Even though they didn't understand the choice, they were supportive and interested in finding a transition plan that worked best for me, best for the business, and ultimately best for them individually. Not in a bad way—in a prudent way. The same can be said for the other key relationships across the broader spectrum of the business: they didn't get it, but they appreciated the choice and were supportive.

I'm still in touch with and respect so many of them for our relationship while I worked there and even more for their demeanor in my transition. It was a complete departure from the worst-case scenario I'd created in my mind. While I'd like to think that each person was disappointed on some level to lose me, their concern in hearing about my exit was not about me as much as it was about continuity—*How are we going to continue to set records now that Dave's done lost his mind and decided to leave?* It was just as transactional as it should have been on their end. And not only that, I see clearly now that I played an important but totally replaceable role. They backfilled me quickly. The team crushed records immediately and every day since, because, of course, I had been a small piece of that big machine.

I let the emotion of my personal relationships and insecurities about my taking a risk cloud the objectivity that they each applied to my departure.

Ego is a funny thing. There's this part of us that believes that if we were to leave a company, leave a relationship, leave a post in life, the people left behind would be devastated about the void we leave in our wake. We believe on some unconscious level that the entire operation will come crashing down if the contributions we've been making aren't available once we're gone. It gives us a sense of self-worth. It makes us feel like the things we're doing are worthy of our time.

Three months after I left Disney, Rachel and I put a movie we made into theaters. It's a fantastic feature-length documentary called *Rachel Hollis Presents: Made for More*. Having been spoiled by my access to the analytics team who could always give me a read on box-office results or the log-on credentials for the systems that show real-time data, I was having withdrawals from the instant gratification that was my old life. So I sent notes to my network of industry connections, asking if they could give me a little insight into what they were seeing.

Silence. Crickets. Nothing.

It took me hours and hours to get a single note back, and the ego in me told me that conspiracy was afoot. The self-important voice that had convinced me of how much I mattered in that role, in the business, was certain that the unreturned e-mails from the execs, producers, and press I'd worked with for years were the product of a secret agreement that I was not to be interacted with. My security clearance had been revoked. As the righteous head of the second-best media company on earth, I was an unknown enemy insurgent. They weren't responding because they were told not to. They agreed not to. *That had to be it.*

My paranoia finally broke me down, and I asked my successor if she'd heard of this industry-wide gag order. If there were some set of hard feelings that were now governing the way the traditional entertainment business responded to me (or didn't).

She laughed. In the nicest way possible. The new leader of my old team laughed out loud at the idea that there was some coordinated effort to keep me out of the know. She assured me in so many words that the industry I left was probably worried about things that were higher on their priority list that day, that they were focused on doing their jobs and not a quick favor for a person who didn't have my old title anymore and who, frankly, could no longer help *them* with a favor in the future.

I can see so clearly now what I couldn't then.

These people I had worked with during my career were amazing, but they were focused on themselves. During my own time on the inside, I had seen thousands of people leave, and when they did, life went on. When they did, I didn't stay connected to the vast majority since they couldn't help me do my job any longer. When it was other people leaving, it made sense to me in a way that I never totally applied to my own departure.

I can say with overwhelming certainty that any worry I had about what people would think of me leaving my job, the industry—it was all unfounded. I'm more than a year removed from having left that great job, and I'm here to tell you that *nobody* cares about what I'm doing now. Yes, they may be watching what we're up to and even enjoying the content we produce, but my worry of being judged by these folks for choosing to do something that made sense to me but maybe not to them—it was a futile exercise in wasted emotion.

Bernard Baruch has a great quote that's often wrongly attributed to Dr. Seuss: "Those who matter don't mind, and those who mind don't matter."[1] If you're holding yourself back because of worry over what other people think, you have to ask yourself if you're giving the right kind of weight to the people in your life to regulate what you do and don't do. There are voices you should listen to, but those voices are few and far between. Don't give up the power you have to be who you were meant to be because of what people who *are not thinking about you* might think.

These people you're worried about? Their fulfillment does not hinge on your success. It's your dream, and because of that you have to make a choice. Are you going to keep people who are just casually a part of your life happy, or are you going to be fulfilled?

If you find yourself struggling to make a move or can't get your motivation for taking that big step you know you need to take, it had better not be because you're holding on to something wrapped in others' opinions. Let it go. Once I was able to push past the worry of what other people might think, I started living my life. Start living yours.

THINGS THAT HELPED ME

1. **I became more intentional with whose thoughts I gave weight to.** I haven't always been as deliberate as

I am now about finding people whose opinions I legitimately respect and whose insights I believe will actually fuel me as a person, Rachel and me as a couple, or our business at large. When you cast the net of whose opinions matter so broadly that it includes *everyone*, it dilutes the power of the opinions that actually do matter. Seeking out experts in our field, friends who have built exceptional relationships, and other people who are committed to personal development allows us to home in on the opinions that might actually help.

2. **I took emotion out of the equation.** My wife is a master at isolating what is real and what is imagined as it pertains to other people's opinions. She's often asking if the thing I'm feeling insecure about is a product of actually hearing someone say something or me assuming that they're thinking a thing that may or may not exist. The emotional side of all of us will contrive a version of events that, when the more objective part of us steps in, often proves not to be true. The more I was able to objectively stand outside of emotion and ask if there was a chance my feelings were fueled by insecurity and not reality, the easier it was to brush that worry aside.

3. **I kept taking unconventional baby steps to gain confidence.** Becoming immune to the opinions of others isn't as easy as just flipping a switch on. For me, finding challenges that pushed me outside my comfort zone and into a space that was less conventional for others created more anxiety the first time I did it. But it became less so each subsequent time. Building confidence is just like training any other muscle. The friction you create is what actually

builds the muscle, and the more you do it, the easier it is to push toward heavier weights. Get yourself into a mindset of trying things that will help you grow even if they don't make sense to other people. This will become your new normal as you take steps, see success, and learn the worth of putting yourself out there. Start small, celebrate your success, and use your growing confidence as the momentum you'll need to push further.

CHAPTER 7

THE LIE:

BEING RIGHT ALL THE TIME DOESN'T MAKE ME AN ASS

Being right all the time totally makes you an ass.

It does. I suffered from this disease of always having to be right in any conversation and all arguments for most of my life. I'm more self-aware of the detrimental side effects today than I've ever been, but, yes, I have to work on it and, yes, now that I recognize the negative impact with better clarity, I don't know how anyone ever put up with it.

As with so many things, the obsession any of us has with being right usually goes way back. For me, so much of it was a by-product of wanting to be accepted, deemed worthy, and loved. Dang it, did I want my parents to think I was perfect. Added to that were the ulcer-inducing anxieties I had about how to fit in and be accepted by my peers at school. And so I honed the unhealthy craft of trying to say and do the things that would show me to be right, of value, accepted, or at the very least not wrong or rejected. This, of course, eventually bled over into professional settings where overarguing became my unconscious attempt to preempt being found out as an under-qualified imposter.

Now that I can look back on all this more clearly, I realize the need to be right always came back to two primary catalysts: fear and ego. *Fear* of what being wrong might say about me at my core, and *ego* driving me to battle for an argument win, regardless of cost. Neither serves me or my relationships. Instead, in a world where I was more comfortable with a good debate, I weaponized my debating strength to a point that it became a weakness over and over in relationships, which was ironic given how it all began with my desire for acceptance.

But here's what I realized: I wasn't always right. You aren't either. I spent so much time associating my ability to win an argument with the affirmation of my value. I held on to positions I'd taken like I was on the back of a bucking bronco, no matter how many new facts might come into the conversation to prove me wrong. I can now appreciate that's a move that actually works to undermine credibility, likability, and value. You can either win every argument and have strained relationships for the rest of your life, or you can humble yourself to the reality that you're not right all the time, accept help when you need it, and change your position when you're presented with new evidence that points in a different direction.

I'm giving this advice to myself as much as you. You see, this fear-ego duo brings out the single greatest and most consistent point of strain in my marriage. My wife isn't confrontational. She doesn't like to argue and isn't up for debate. I've used this knowledge in a way I convinced myself was to my advantage over time. It wasn't. If you're in pursuit of an exceptional relationship with your partner and still find yourself falling into the trap of needing to be right, it won't work to your advantage either.

It's taken a decade and a half of marriage to appreciate that my preying on her discomfort in arguments may have fed my ego or helped suppress my fear, but it came at the expense of showing up well for her. If I'm really honest, using my ability to win an argument with a person who is adverse to arguing made me a bully. The worst kind of ass. Don't be that guy.

I'll confess this is what happened when my wife first handed me that draft of *Girl, Wash Your Face*. I was absolutely positive she needed to change most of it. I knew I was right. I made my case over and over again. I said it in a way that made it seem like I knew what I was talking about. I used that same hubris I'd won countless arguments with over time. I made that face—that "I'm 100 percent positive" face.

Thankfully, I failed in swaying my jury of one and, thankfully, I was proven very wrong.

For those of you who are unfamiliar, *Girl, Wash Your Face* is a book about how my wife, Rachel, struggled with anxiety and alcohol and shame and grief and me. She talked about all the things. In detail. Specifically, those chapters about me, about our relationship, those were the ones that particularly felt like they had no good place in the book. Reading it fueled so much insecurity in me, and I was emphatic that it was pulling on the wrong threads.

I mean, what in the world? Think about the worst things

you've ever done to your partner or the parts of your life that you're not necessarily proud of. Now imagine that partner wrote about them, in detail, in a book that would live on shelves forever and ever. For anyone to read.

What would the people at my office think? What about my family, or hers? How would we handle the comments from strangers on the internet? It now seems so silly.

Having read literally thousands of notes from the millions of people who've read her book, I now know that the stories she included afforded the audience comfort, a feeling of shared experiences, an encouraging voice of hope. That book was a tool that allowed those who read it to fundamentally take control of their lives and change them for the better.

I wrote this in the aftermath of my wife's book becoming a number one *New York Times* bestseller. When I typed these words, it had been on that list for sixty-seven consecutive weeks and was only bumped from its number one perch by her follow-up book, *Girl, Stop Apologizing*, when it debuted at number one a little more than a year later. Rachel's willingness to resist my declarations that I knew what was best for her and her book is the secret sauce to why it went on to sell about three million copies in the first year.

In the end, it was *because of* her vulnerability and the empathy it brought about, because of how universal those stories were, that her book finished as the second biggest seller of 2018 behind Michelle Obama's *Becoming*. It connected across ages, religious affiliation, voter history, folks working or not, with kids or not, even female or not. In fact, I wrote this book you're currently reading because I was proven so wrong. The evidence of what happened when she started owning her stories

pushed me to start believing in the power of honestly owning mine.

Exposing the lie in this case meant eating a delicious serving
of crow. Being right all the time did make me an ass and would
have cost us the opportunity for massive, global impact if not
for my wife sticking to her guns.

It's simple. For the sake of your personal brand, your ability
to connect in a relationship, and maybe even a book the world
needs to read, get out of your own way and allow yourself to be
wrong when you are.

THINGS THAT HELPED ME

1. **I prioritized which hills to take.** Losing some battles
   to win the war is a thing. Even in the instances when I
   felt like I was absolutely right, fighting for that position
   on a topic that really didn't matter wasn't worth the col-
   lateral damage it might do to a relationship long-term.
   Not all arguments are created equal. The sooner you can
   appreciate that there are some things not worth fighting
   for, the better you'll use your time. Work on building your
   relationships up for the times when you really do need to
   take a stand on something that actually matters.

2. **I saw the downside of insisting I was "right" when
   I was "wrong."** When I put myself in the shoes of the
   person on the other side of my arguing and thought about
   how they might receive my unrelenting debate, it gave me
   pause. I've been the person stifling the eye roll as I listen to someone insist that he's right, and I have seen the

unwillingness to be wrong as a sign of insecurity, imma-
turity, or both. When I learned to ask myself if I might be
seen that way, the answer demanded a yield and a pivot.

3. **I opened myself to the value of others' ideas.** There
is an upside to considering other people's ideas and points
of view as you tackle an issue. Once I was able to move
past the association that being wrong in an argument was
something that made me less as a person, active listening became an option. When you value achieving the goal
over being right about the best way to get there, you not
only get there faster because of the new possibilities you've
opened yourself up to, you've likely endeared yourself to
your partner or team who have become accomplices in
getting you there.

CHAPTER 8

THE LIE:

FAILURE MEANS YOU'RE WEAK

A couple of years ago, my oldest son, Jackson, came to me and asked for my thoughts on his running for president of his elementary school class. We had a good conversation about it in part because I had some experience in this department. Not once, but twice I'd run for president of different classes. I liked the hustle of having to work hard to convince people to vote for me. I liked the challenge of trying to win, especially against the backdrop of not wanting to be embarrassed if I were to lose. It was an exhilarating risk to take.

I lost both times I ran. Good stuff. It was humiliating and disappointing and hard to deal with the feeling that I must not have been good enough or didn't work hard enough or hadn't been likable enough. Something in the "enough" department felt like it was lacking in that real-time processing of the losses, but in both cases, I look back now and see how powerfully important those losses were for me in how I grew into who I'd become. It was through that lens that I immediately insisted Jackson go for it.

His first question was, "Should I run?" I gave the emphatic "Yes!"

His second question was, "What if I lose?" Without missing a beat, I challenged him with a higher-pitched "So what if you lose?!"

With that, he decided to run, and the platform "Stronger Together" was born. Posters were made. Campaigning kicked off. He wrote and delivered a speech to the student body. He felt confident of his chances to win.

On the eve of the election, I found myself in the strange position of weighing which outcome I was actually rooting for. Of course I like the idea of seeing my kids set goals, work toward each one, and achieve them—there are great lessons in that and great confidence that can be built from showing yourself that you can achieve the things you set your mind to. That, combined with the natural feelings of a dad who wants to protect his child from having to experience pain and rejection, made the answer easy: *we're pulling for a win.* But, when I thought about what would provide more meaning in Jackson's life, what might best prepare him for his future, what might give him the skills of perseverance and prove a point that trying and failing wouldn't kill him, the answer changed. Even though it might hurt, the thing he likely needed most was to not get the thing he wanted.

Jackson put everything into that campaign, but he still lost. It was hard for him to deal with the tendency we all have to feel embarrassed about public defeat, but it proved to be an incredibly rich moment and an opportunity for me as a dad to teach some very valuable lessons.

- Failing at something doesn't make you a failure—not as a student, not in life, and certainly not as my son.
- You never lose when you fail; you only learn from the experience.
- The best growth comes from learning from things you fail at.
- The opinions of people sitting on the sidelines should not intimidate you, because you've already done something they haven't by putting yourself in the game.

Ironically, at the time we were having this conversation I was stuck in the middle of that funk where my own inability to fail was causing so much discontent. To be clear, that inability to fail was because the movies and team and brands I was working on in those days were just too good to fail, too strong to put me in positions where I could really make mistakes I could learn from. There was very little risk involved. In some ways, my son running for president and losing reminded me of the power of putting yourself in a position to fail . . . so you will.

The decisions I made in the years after those failed elementary school presidential campaigns—in particular, leaving certainty to join Rachel in building the Hollis Company—were in part an attempt to force myself into situations where I could fail so I could grow. I know with absolute certainty that, on the whole, we're going to succeed. I know with that same degree of certainty that because I've leaped into something I don't know how to do, I'm most likely going to fail on an hourly basis here at the beginning. Even though there are days when I have to work a little more to remember that these failures are for me and for my growth, the sense of fulfillment that comes from what I learn every time I fall on my face is extraordinary.

How you process failure, it turns out, is all about mindset. And mindset is everything. The authority on this is Carol Dweck and her book *Mindset*. Finish this book, but then read that one next. It's the best work available on this topic, and if you're new to thinking about how your mind functions, how you process failure, I promise it's worth having your mind blown by this PhD's work.

In the most basic terms, Dweck tells us there are two types of people in the world. Those who believe they were born with a certain amount of talent, gifts, and ability (those are the *fixed-mindset* folk, like I was for so many years of my life), and those who believe they can continue to grow into what they have in talents, skills, and abilities by learning and surrounding them-selves with smarter people (those are *growth-mindset* folk). The fixed-mindset person thinks outcomes are predetermined and as a result may plateau early and achieve less than their full potential. The growth-mindset person believes that what's possible for their life sits more in their hands, and as a result they will go out and achieve more for believing it.[1]

This was a concept I'd never given any real consideration to before, but once I started to think about it, I realized that, unless you're paying attention to it, *the way you think may be leading you, rather than you leading the way you think*. That's a massive deal in a single sentence. Another way to think about it is to ask yourself, are you actively pursuing a mindset that serves you, or are you being controlled by one you haven't really given much thought to?

If you're in a season where you feel stuck, I'm going to guess your experience has been more like it was for me for the better part of the last five years, operating without much thought about how your mind works or what your mind suggests you can or can't do. Until I sat up and took notice, I lived as a victim of my unconscious rather than a commander of my mind and focus.

In some ways, my fixed mindset was a by-product of my results. I was a competent guy who got good grades and could talk his way out of trouble. When I did well, I attributed it to having been born with gifts that made it possible. I was raised in a faith community that told us we were made perfectly by a God who envisioned who we would be long before we were born; and, in believing that, I inferred that there were some things I was born ready to do and other things I just wasn't created to do. Would reaching beyond the things that came easy even occur to me with that mentality? Never. Not ever.

So, for the great part of my adult life, I pushed into areas where I knew I'd excel and avoided terrain that might create challenges. I took jobs I knew I could crush and only made myself vulnerable in relationships where I knew I couldn't get hurt. So often I played it safe in a way that cooked the books in my favor. If there was a chance I wouldn't be great, I tended to avoid or, even worse, self-sabotage in order to avoid being tested or exposed as one who still needed work. When it looked like it might take time to learn something, I avoided taking the time required. And when things got hard, I'd give up to find something I could conquer more quickly.

The result? I affirmed I had talent in the areas I was most comfortable in, but that affirmation came at the expense of actually acquiring new knowledge. The avoidance of failure to preserve the optics of strength came with the trade-off of not adding new tools to my toolbox in a way that would have made me grow.

It's been said that at the end of your life you will be more disappointed by the things that you didn't do than the things that you did do. I've come around to believe that to be true. John Shedd put it another way: "A ship in harbor is safe, but that's not what ships are built for."[2] I resonate so much with this that it's a tattoo I now wear on my right forearm. It acts as a reminder to me and my kids to always be testing the choppy waters outside our comfort zone—where growth shows up.

My wife's been on this growth-mindset train since day one. How did she build her company, become the mogul she is, and create the expertise that has led to her teaching from stages and being a number one *New York Times* bestselling author? She did it by unapologetically putting herself over and over in situations where she might fail, where she might learn something from her mistakes and grow. She's not ashamed of asking questions and actively pursuing answers anytime she doesn't know the "how" to any problem she is up against. Her example has changed the way I think about the vulnerability required to admit you don't have it all together and that you need the help of another to get from where you are to where you want to be. Her willingness to pursue dreams that might end in failure, to get back up and seek more knowledge when it does? That's the game changer. Hello.

In the end, whether it's Jackson, me, or you, the most important takeaway here is realizing the immense value in reengineering your brain to appreciate the benefit and necessity of failure. Today's culture has demonized failure, which means it's on each of us to reframe it in a positive light as something you absolutely have to have if you want a rich, full life that continues to be better tomorrow than today. It means measuring success against a set of criteria tied not to how little you fail but how fast you get back up, how much you learn when you stumble, how the resources you needed to solve your mistakes have become part of your arsenal going forward.

As a dad, I'm continually putting my kids in situations where they can fail. I root for them to win as much as I privately hope they lose. I want them to build confidence from their wins, but I also want them to normalize trying things they don't do well at so it never occurs to them that failure is a bad thing. As I teach them, I have to remind myself of these same lessons, especially on the days when our company has a shipping snafu, or a system breaks, or one of the hundred other problems that will crop up before lunch. But as soon as it feels like we've gotten the hang of our problems, or the opportunity to fail feels like it's been solved and no longer drives personal and organizational growth, well, that will be the time for us to take on a new kind of business we've never tried before, so we can start failing and learning all over again.

THINGS THAT HELPED ME

1. **I found the clear connection between stability and unfulfillment.** As a person who'd put an extraordinary priority on stability and certainty, when that very thing I'd considered so important became a prison that kept me from fully using my potential, I could see that my understanding of how things worked needed to change. If certainty

led to unfulfillment, uncertainty must lead to fulfillment. I started testing that hypothesis and, sure enough, in seasons of uncertainty, though they invited more failures, the growth that came from that lack of safe stability produced more wins.

2. **I looked for examples of people who'd failed their way to success.** It may sound crazy, but it's not a difficult search. For every business you respect, every CEO you admire, almost every time their story shows how they're now standing on top of layer after layer of failures, not successes. Familiarize yourself with as many stories like this as possible, and you will take the stigma of failure and turn it on its head, making it seem as though real success isn't possible without failure—since it's not.

3. **I forced myself to say yes to things that made me feel uncomfortable.** In this new enterprise of ours, vulnerability is a daily requirement with live streams and podcasts and book writing. Transitioning from a world where I was cautious about how much of my real self I showed made most of these things feel very hard at first, as I worried about failing at something new. This move into unbelievable transparency has become strangely normal and, over time, easier to do. I'm not saying you should start doing what I do every day, but if you're worried about failing as a public speaker, get out and speak. Don't love to sell? Pick up the phone and fail at making a sale twenty-five times before you get a sale on the twenty-sixth. Want to get into shape but don't know how to start? Start, fail, learn, repeat. It gets easier, whatever *it* is.

CHAPTER 9

THE LIE:

IT'S MY JOB TO PROTECT THEM FROM PROBLEMS

When Rachel gets upset, my very first instinct is, *What can I do to fix this?* As in right away, before too much time passes and she experiences more discomfort than is absolutely necessary. It's wired into my being, the role I feel I'm supposed to play to keep her happy, to keep my kids from experiencing pain, the desire I have to maintain equilibrium in my home at all times. I'm a peacekeeper by nature, and keeping the peace, managing expectations so people aren't let down, alleviating pain when it comes up . . . those are my jobs. At least I thought they were.

We went through a crazy 2016. As part of an adoption journey that was rolling into the third year of a five-year ride, we'd moved from a failed international adoption into the Los Angeles County foster-to-adopt world. We were so naive about this. We didn't realize we were making an intentional choice that would introduce problems for our family at a rate never previously experienced. Problems I thought I had to fix. Problems I couldn't fix. You see, "problems," it turns out, may not exist for me to fix in the first place, and it took inviting more problems than we could have ever imagined for me to learn that it's not my job to fix them or prevent them from happening.

Foster care is hard. Sadly, the system is broken and built on the back of tragedy. And even though we'll fight for the rest of our lives to help mend that brokenness and support the families who provide care for these children so badly in need of consistency and love, the reality of foster care was nothing we could have fully understood until we were all the way in. It was April 2016 when we got the news that a baby girl was being placed with us. In the middle of our excitement, I also remember the overwhelming urge to make sure we didn't get too attached. I wanted to control how much it might disrupt our bio kids. I needed it to make sense to our extended family, to make sure we told folks at our jobs the right stories so they understood our "why." And then an eleven-month-old baby was dropped at our house by a stranger in a white van with a pillowcase of belongings and a wish of good luck. *Ummm.*

Our family went from five to six in the matter of a phone call and thirty-eight minutes of drive time. It was crazy and surreal, and two days later we got a call that our first placement's twenty-two-month-old sister also needed a home. In the blink of an eye, we were saying yes to being a family of seven. Double *ummm.* We couldn't have anticipated in those early days the collective thirty-three months of trauma these precious babies came into our home with and how it would intermittently show up, the unreal mix of emotions that would come during biological parent visits, and how odd it felt to invite social workers into our home.

It was controlled chaos. No. It was chaos. It was beautifully hard and a window into a world that desperately needed love. Walking into it softened some of the edges of our hearts. The experience helped us appreciate the small things we found ourselves fortunate to have.

That initial foster placement was a mix of beauty and challenge, but it was the first step in a process we had unwittingly entered. We wanted to adopt a daughter, and we'd found out after we were too far down the road that, in order to adopt in the county of Los Angeles, we needed to foster first. It was a requirement. A prerequisite. A thing they forgot to mention until the seventy-fourth hour of a seventy-five-hour parenting class that we thought would get us certified. Foster care? For us? Full-time working parents of three humans already? This journey seemed to be taking on a life of its own after our international adoption attempt in Ethiopia hadn't worked out. And now we held on for the ride. Adoption was what we felt called into, and foster care was the road required to get there.

Every single part of me wanted to stop it before it started. How many unforeseen problems would we be opening ourselves up to? Why would we intentionally agree to do something that felt so hard and came with so many scenarios that disrupted our lives? How would we pull it off with everything else we had going on? What about our boys?

Every instinct I had to cut problems off at the pass was

activated at the news that we were going to be foster parents. In nature's style of fight-or-flight impulses, the "flight" button was flashing red hot. It felt so big and overwhelming, so we decided to stop thinking of all that could go wrong and instead focused on all that could go right. We decided to fight for our daughter and ask more positive "what if" questions.

What if fostering got us closer to our adopted daughter joining us forever?

What if it let us help a baby who needed us in that moment?

What if it modeled for our boys how to love, even when it's unconventional or hard?

So we dived in. We welcomed these precious girls and their trauma and their smiles and the looks they gave each other in their being kept together. We hosted a one-year-old birthday party and a two-year-old birthday party, our friends and family making a big deal out of a couple of little people they didn't really know, who we didn't really know. We helped a baby take her first steps and say her first words and worked with a system that didn't feel normal but hadn't yet revealed its full brokenness. This toe-dip into uncertainty and ignoring the flashing red light of "flight" felt good. The girls were with us for three months. When they were ready for their return home, we kissed them goodbye and then turned the corner into our happy ending, finding the forever daughter we'd adopt in the next stage of our journey.

Sure. Well, actually, no. It wasn't anything like that.

That would have been nice. Or would it?

It was two months after our now one- and two-year-old first placements left our home. The phone rang at work around 3:00 p.m. on a Thursday afternoon in July as I was doing what

I was normally doing: having a meeting . . . about an upcoming meeting. My assistant walked in and said it was Rachel and it sounded urgent. I hurried to my desk.

"Everyone's okay. I got a call from the county. They have babies we can adopt . . . immediately."

Hello. What? Did you say "babies," as in more than one human? The idea that "everyone's okay" felt misplaced.

We jumped on the phone with an emergency placement worker and got the details: "They're four-day-old twins. Their mother left the hospital in the middle of the night. This is your opportunity for fast-track adoption. If you can do this, they can keep them together rather than place them in separate homes tomorrow. You should know, they're being weaned from cocaine in their system, so it will be a bit of work at first. Oh, and they need to know in twenty minutes."

Making that decision in those twenty minutes is something we will point to twenty-five years from now as a critical domino in so many things that would follow.

Twins are hard. Twins being weaned off drugs are even harder. We could have never imagined what we were signing up for on top of three other kids, two full-time jobs, navigating the county of Los Angeles, and attempting to learn all we could about their culture (the babies were African American and we're Caucasian) to take proper care of their skin and hair and connection to community.

We got off the phone with the social worker and said a long "what should we do" prayer. Our home was certified for two kids from that first placement, which felt ordained. We had a community ready to help, friends who'd adopted multiple kids before, and an intentionally multicultural church. These all felt like things that had been placed in our lives to prepare us to answer in the affirmative when someone gives you twenty minutes to agree to something so big.

So we said yes.

That first month was a blur. Sleep didn't really exist, and if it did it happened during strange hours in unconventional places, and never synced with anyone else's. It was exhausting and hard and the happiest I think I've ever seen my wife. Our family was complete, our adoption journey done, these babies that we picked up at the hospital and named and sleeplessly kept alive for a month were thriving, starting to get into a rhythm. Our chaos was slowly turning to normalcy. They were ours, we were us, it was good.

And then it wasn't.

We got a call about five weeks in, telling us that the outreach that fateful Thursday afternoon, the call that had represented the adoptability of these babies and had given us twenty minutes to decide, had turned out to have been a misrepresentation. A story. A thing that a desperate emergency social worker had said, thinking it was a likely scenario that would play out, not knowing there was a biological family member petitioning the courts in the background for custody. Custody of our daughters. Well. *Our daughters* is a misnomer. They weren't ours. They never were.

I thought the call in July was the one that would change our lives. In truth, the call in July was the disruption we chose. The call in August was the disruption that chose us.

The next few weeks were brutal. We were given the breakdown of how a judge would hear a case, how things usually go in these proceedings, how the twins might be able to stay, but how, if these social workers explaining things were honest, they'd likely have to leave our home. The rest of the world did not exist. We felt broken and scared and confused. That light started flashing again: "Flight, Flight, Flight." *Protect Rachel. Protect your boys. Protect yourself. Protect your broken hearts.*

I was numb.

Rachel was gutted.

A few weeks later, that same white van that had dropped off two baby girls in the spring was back to drive off with two baby girls in the fall. It happened in the blink of an eye. It happened with little fanfare or emotion from the woman who nonchalantly put them in their car seats and threw a nice but unconvincing wave. They were gone. We were shattered. Rachel was done.

The aftermath of the twins leaving wasn't pretty. Our boys watched as we modeled true sadness. Rachel and I were in the bottom of a trench, clinging to each other, just trying to survive. It didn't feel like it in real time, but it took the hardest thing we'd ever been through to see how strong we could be for each other. It took enduring this impossible season to appreciate our ability to endure *any* impossible season that gets thrown our way in the future. I thought I knew we were strong. I thought I knew we could make it through anything. Actually doing it made those thoughts of how strong and resilient we *could* be look so small compared to what I believe today on the other side.

Our boys? They were having their mettle tested as well. Resiliency wasn't a trait they'd been formally introduced to; it wasn't something we'd even really thought about exposing them to. I can see now that I'd gone out of my way to make sure they didn't ever find themselves in situations they'd have to be resilient through.

Our faith? Tested. Really tested. In fact, only when we found ourselves throwing our hands in the air and asking why it felt like we'd been led into a place only to be left there were we able to truly understand faith. It's easy to believe when things are going well. Believing while they're going terribly wrong—that was something I'd never truly been forced to do.

It took this experience to change my thinking. As hard as it was to watch, the impossibility of fixing what was happening in our lives showed us the incredible power of enduring, proving to us as a family that we were up for it all. We came out the other side stronger, even though it required discomfort and tears and uncertainty.

The idea of pulling ourselves up and going back to "normal" lives was hard to wrap our heads around. It didn't feel possible, but a couple of weeks after the twins left we found ourselves out in the backyard, stuck in the conversation we'd been in since they left: "How do we move forward?" Rachel had been the driver of the conversation around adoption up to that point, but our roles had shifted, and I said something so uncharacteristic of me and a lifetime of wanting to prevent us from experiencing pain. I said we needed to keep going in this pursuit of a daughter, that *our desire for a daughter didn't go away just because it got hard.*

In that moment, rather than trying to prevent pain, I was trying to prevent us from having to live with *regret.* I could so clearly see the ten-years-removed version of ourselves mourning the daughter who never became part of our family. This hard, impossible season would come and go, but that feeling of an unfinished family would float as a cloud above us forever. I knew it felt hard to continue this push, but in that backyard on that day, I also knew with certainty that the trade-off of short-term pain would be nothing compared to the permanence of not trying.

So we transitioned onto the path toward independent adoption and made an appointment with an attorney. It was a Friday in November when we met with him to learn about the unconventionally beautiful process that is private adoption, but on Wednesday of that same week Rachel asked me to reach out to the twins' biological dad to see if we could bring him some food, bring them some clothes, do something, anything to help with the closure we were looking for so desperately.

So I called him. We had a very pleasant conversation.

He politely declined.

He didn't want anything to do with us and didn't want us in his daughters' lives. We were on the other side of what would have been a battle for custody, so it was hard for him to appreciate the rationale behind our request.

I understood.

I knew Rachel would be broken by the news. Again.

Then that Friday meeting came, and it went well. After four hours of learning all about a somewhat foreign process, we left feeling good about the decision, about the road ahead, that we had a plan and a restored hope in a dream that had felt hopeless for some time. As luck would have it, the office of the attorney was next door to an amazing restaurant that we'd been to a couple of times in celebration. It was a Beverly Hills joint where they sell twenty-two-dollar-grilled-cheese sandwiches, but it felt like overpriced bread and cheese was perfectly appropriate for the step we'd just successfully taken.

We sat outside, overlooking a fountain and overhearing the ridiculous conversations that you cross your fingers for when you come to a place like this: highest-class problems, the eye roll-inducing complaints of day-drinking socialites. It was perfect.

And then Rachel asked, "Hey, did you get in touch with the twins' dad about us bringing over some food?"

I'd known the answer for two days and had decided to keep it to myself so we could actually make it to the meeting with our attorney. Now, though, I made that scrunched-up-nose look and said, "He doesn't want us to be involved."

Tears.

Rachel was wearing a very stylish pair of Jackie O sunglasses. You know, the kind that covers the majority of your face. But when those words dropped out of my mouth, her tears came streaming down. Not like a gentle cry. This was a full-on gut-punch, and she was sent back in that instant to the moment we had gotten the news of the twins' un-adoptable-ness. She composed herself long enough to say two words through heavy sobbing that I'll never forget: "I'm done."

My compelling argument in our backyard was one thing, but this time I didn't think I could change her mind. This wasn't about the last four hours of a meeting being wiped out; this was the choice to end the marathon that was this ever-changing slog to adopt a daughter. Rachel was done, and in the moment, I was with her.

The tables at this twenty-two-dollar-grilled-cheese restaurant were incredibly close to each other. Close enough that, when the man at the table next to us slammed his hand down on our table, it startled us both out of our tears.

"You can't give up," he told us emphatically. We both stared at him dumbfounded. "I'm so sorry to interrupt," he told us, "but I couldn't help but overhear. I was adopted. My parents had failed adoptions before they adopted me and my brother, and they sat in the place that you're sitting now and had to make a choice to give up or keep going. They kept going. If they hadn't kept going I wouldn't be here. If they hadn't kept going I wouldn't have graduated at the top of my class or married my wife or have my career. You can't quit. I think I'm sitting here right now, because I'm supposed to tell you that you can't give up."

Our jaws were on the floor.

We wiped away our tears and reached out our hands to officially introduce ourselves to the stranger sitting next to us. He responded with two more words I'll never forget: "I'm Noah." Of course, his name was Noah. Of course, in the flood we were experiencing, we were sent a Noah to help us appreciate that we needed to go on, and that, in a sea of doubt that truly tested our faith, God had been with us the entire time.

We decided to not give up.

November became January, and we were paired with a pregnant mama looking for adoptive parents for her baby. At the end of February, she gave birth with us in the room to welcome our baby girl. When the nurse asked us for a name, there was only one that felt like a fit: Noah. Noah Elizabeth. Noah, for the original Noah who trusted and built despite the lack of evidence for the impending flood, as well as the Noah at the restaurant who had encouraged us to have faith at a time when the path didn't feel safe or certain. And Elizabeth, the middle name shared by my wife and the wonderfully selfless woman who chose to trust us with her baby. It was a happy ending to our nearly five-year journey.

I did a podcast recently telling our story, and when I was done the interviewer said, "I'm so sorry that you and your family went through this." Here's the thing: I'm not. I used to think that way. When we were in the middle of it, we would have loved for everything to go as planned, pain-free and happy. But now, on the other side of things, I'm not sorry it all happened. In fact, I'm happy it happened—exactly as it did. I'm proud we made choices that created massive disruption in our lives. I'm grateful that the decisions we made and the forces that interceded in our life to turn it completely upside down did just what they did.

Even as it caused pain and discomfort and tears.

Because it caused pain and discomfort and tears. Lots of tears.

As much as I never want to live through the end of 2016 again, I find myself grateful. I'm happy I didn't find a way to keep the painful things from happening. I appreciate the tests and lessons that afforded us strength as individuals, as a couple, and as a family. In fact, one of the most important lessons was coming to see that the critical things that will shape who we are and how we'll grow as a family will only get enough oxygen to do so when we stop trying to fix them and allow them to happen. Much of what my kids need to become the people they are meant to be requires them to endure things they may not like. And being a good partner to my wife isn't exclusively about preventing discomfort, but standing alongside her when she goes through a hard time or needs support after a long day.

Whether it's me personally, my support of my wife, or my parenting my kids, many times what I need most is to not get what I want. Growing through those difficult seasons allows us to come out stronger, more mature, more confident in our ability to handle whatever comes next. Are you a peacekeeper? Resist the temptation to fix everything. First, you can't actually do it. Second, if you can, it may very well keep you and your family from seeing what that challenge was meant to pull out of you as you become a bigger version of yourself.

THINGS THAT HELPED ME

1. **I sought counsel from other people who'd been there.** Resisting the temptation to fix things that could disrupt our life required first finding those who could tell me how they survived the same kind of season in theirs, how they maneuvered through it, how they were stronger coming out the other end. When something comes up that you reflexively reach to fix, ask if you know anyone else who is successfully navigating that problem or is on the other side of resolution. The positive proof that came from knowing that others had been there first was critical in our foster-adoption journey, but it is just as important to find positive examples of how other husbands process stresses with their wives or how other dads approach discipline or rewards with their kids.

2. **I stopped fixing small things to train my caveman brain.** We have a kind of brain in our heads that has, from the beginning of time, been about survival—and that survival sometimes required man to hunt and gather to provide for a family that waited for his return to eat. That centuries-old brain meets ego and societal gender norms in a place that tells men it's our job to fix everything. That primal wiring, those pangs of ego swimming against the current in culture, they require baby-stepping through

times when you don't hunt and don't gather. When you allow those loved ones you'd normally fix things for to show that they can survive without your fixing things for them, they might actually thrive. Let your son crash on the bike (with a helmet), and let him dust himself off. Let your wife vent about a challenging day, and do only what she needs most: listen. Practicing this with the small things will give you the confidence and boldness to do the same when life presents a disruption you can't fix or one where good comes from living through it.

3. **I visualized the outcome, not the problem.** When we wanted to teach our boys to become more independent, take responsible risks, and respect their elders, we sent them away. We sent them to camp. It challenged the idea that I alone was responsible for helping them become who I hope they grow into. Shocking to my ego, yes, but so important for me to learn. I started with what I wanted them to be—independent, responsible, and respectful— and worked backward to how to accomplish that, which, in this case, was sending them off to camp. It's the same for my marriage, my relationships with employees, or friends. My fixing their problems has sometimes been the problem, and it took knowing what I ultimately wanted out of the relationship to pull me out of their way for their good.

CHAPTER 10

THE LIE:

I CAN PHONE IT IN AND BE JUST FINE

I was a telemarketer in high school. I apologize if you were one of the lucky people I called to tell that you may have already won a European dream vacation or one of ten other fabulous prizes, but I needed the money. The job paid in two ways: you made a small amount for each call you made and a bigger amount for every person you sold into some kind of time-share vacation club. Converting a sale was hard, so I literally *phoned it in*. I made as many calls as I could, read my script, accepted their no, and did it over again until the end of my shift.

It was the worst.

My job satisfaction was a reflection of my effort.

Just as I reached my breaking point, one of the more seasoned salesmen asked if he could give me some tips. He helped with my pitch and showed me the way to personalize the sale, the way to work through objections and turn a *no* into a *yes*.

It was simple, it built confidence, and, incredibly, it worked. Most importantly, it challenged the way sixteen-year-old me connected the effort I put into something with the result that comes from it.

I've had to push myself not to default to a path of least resistance my entire life. Just because I can pass this test without having to try as hard, will I get as much out of this class without studying? Even if my boss would be happy with me giving a 70 percent effort, might I feel a greater sense of satisfaction and grow more by leaning in with all I have? Though I could get away with letting the kids sit on technology all weekend while Rachel's out of town, what would it look like to push into being an exceptional dad who is actively present rather than being satisfied with us just surviving her time away?

As a person who's had far too much practice over the years doing the bare minimum to get by, I can tell you it's no way to live. Not using your full potential, putting in complete effort, working hard to see the fruit of your labor? That's a recipe for unfulfillment of the highest order.

That's treading water day after day.

Tread water long enough and you're bound to go under.

I had the surreal benefit of sitting in a room with Steve Jobs one time before he passed away. Dressed in his classic all black and speaking with a steady confidence that could only come from the genius founder of Apple, he left an indelible mark on my life in the course of a sixty-minute meeting.

In its simplest form, the main takeaway he dropped was

something to this effect: every time you interact with anyone, you either make a positive brand deposit or a negative brand withdrawal. That's the case whether you think about how people receive you personally or how they receive your product. If you're good and have a quality interaction, it produces a deposit that reinforces the quality impression you're hoping the audience leaves with. If you're not so good, it acts as a brand withdrawal, giving people an impression of you that will leave them questioning if you are as advertised, if you're a person or product they should place their trust in.

We all have times when we know we're on, when we're auditioning for the next great opportunity, doing the work to get that promotion, or attempting to get that next job. What most of us don't give as much thought to is the real-time reality that we're in a perpetual state of being evaluated by the folks around us. Every single interaction we have is an opportunity to either leave someone feeling better or worse about you or your product. Like, all the time.

This isn't about giving weight to other people's opinions and adjusting your course to meet them at the expense of who you want to be. This is being conscious at all times of how your actions and your hoped-for reception align to deliver the personal brand you aspire to. That alignment is your integrity: having principles that are reflected in every interaction.

There will be times when it feels like we can just "phone it in," when we can do as little as is required because nobody's really looking (at least nobody who really matters). That's rarely the case. The idea that there won't be an impact is confronted with reality on the regular: everyone we interact with is either having a deposit or withdrawal kind of experience with us. As a father of younger boys, I've often had to explain this notion of "integrity" as something that happens when no one else is watching—the way we would hope to behave if the secret shopper of our life were to surprise us by looking in when we were least expecting it.

But, actually, there's always someone watching. It may be your kids who will follow your model; it may be that person in the meeting who one day becomes a hiring manager considering you for the next big job. The bottom line is your willingness to show up consistently. The brand you want people to think of when asked about you must be consistent with your actions.

Years ago we heard a message at church that was an absolute mind-blower. The kind of sermon you end up taking back into every circle of your life because it fundamentally changed the way you think. Our pastor taught on the difference between being a thermostat and being a thermometer. It was a sermon I've preached to every team I've had since.

A thermometer is something that reacts to the temperature in a room. When it's hot, it goes up; when it's cold, it goes down. It only reacts. A thermostat, on the other hand, is something you set to dictate the sought-after temperature in a room. You want it warm; you set it warm. You want it cool; you set it cool. It's proactive about achieving specific results.

So if you're serious about establishing a reputation that matches your character, whether in your career or in your private relationships, trust me, you want to be a thermostat. You want to be someone who is intentional with their actions and how they move you toward that brand, rather than simply reacting, turning on when those rare situations demand it but coasting mindlessly otherwise.

How do you actively choose to be a thermostat of a person?

You have to start with a question: *What is the outcome I'm looking for?* I've had the opportunity to work on two projects with Oprah Winfrey. (Dang it, that feels like a name drop in a chapter that also includes Steve Jobs, but push past any gag reflex and go with me here.) In each instance, whenever we started a meeting, she asked a simple question: "What is the intended outcome of this meeting?" I mean, my intended outcome was a selfie, but that's another story for another time. The simplicity of that question guided the way, and we would do just about everything in that meeting to ensure we arrived at the intended outcome.

When was the last time you asked what the outcome of the interaction in front of you might be? When you're a thermometer, just phoning it in and letting things happen, sure, you may appear as you hope to every now and then—in the same way a broken clock is right twice a day. But that won't get you very far. If you don't want to only be a good parent when the conditions are right, or only be a great boss when the situation affords it easily, take control of how you set the temperature you need to get the outcome you're looking for. In focusing on the end goal of how you want to be received, you'll approach every interaction deliberately, and the situational distractions of life won't throw you off your game. You won't unintentionally present in a way that doesn't serve you or the intended outcome. Instead, you'll more consistently produce the results you're interested in and be more ready to navigate the unexpected, which you should absolutely expect will come up.

Can you phone it in now and then? You can . . . but at what cost? When you know your personal brand could be audited at any time by anyone, you will choose to show up more consistently. Your actions and outcomes will be aligned. And in that consistency and alignment, you will elicit the response you're hoping for more often.

But even beyond the outside audit, consider the impact of the internal audit as well. How will knowing you pushed yourself into an uncomfortable space and survived make you think differently about a challenge the next time it presents itself? When you see the callus on your palm from the hard work you put in, what might that sense of satisfaction in knowing you gave your all make you feel?

At the end of the day, not phoning it in is as much about the person looking back at you in the mirror as it is about the way the outside world receives your effort. Push yourself to consistently be your very best, and you will grow a sense of pride and self-respect that redefines who you think you are and what you think you're capable of. If you go all in, this new sense of self acts as a catalyst to propel you forward in every part of your life. Let's go.

THINGS THAT HELPED ME

1. **I got specific about the details of my personal brand.**
   If I only had sixty seconds to make sure you knew who I am and what I stand for, I feel confident I could communicate it in the ascent of a single elevator ride. I've done the work to know what it is I want people to take away from interacting with me. Because I'm clear on that, I can work on a regular basis to make sure my actions support and align with that vision. Consider too the *whole person* when getting into your specifics. Though Steve Jobs's wisdom was an insight in this chapter, he's ironically renowned for

not only his prolific genius in business and marketing but also for his rough edges interpersonally. Finding balance in all aspects of your brand matters.

2. **I made a list of the "operating principles" for delivering consistent brand deposits.** If you were to describe how you hope to be in your life, could you list the ten things you would need to do consistently to have people describe you in that way? We hit this concept of operating principles at the end of the book, but basically it's the idea that if you set guidelines and stay consistent to them, any person who drops in on your life would see you in the way you'd hope. I start with what I want my brand to be, then ask what it will take to act in a way that reinforces that.

3. **I remind myself that you just never know.** Once, while I was in the middle of pitching a new piece of business, I looked up and noticed a single face that looked so familiar. I couldn't place him, and it wasn't until we were almost done with the meeting that this person let me in on the mystery of where we'd met before. Across the table from me was someone I'd worked with years ago whom I'd fortunately befriended, even though he'd been a difficult cat to work with. I felt grateful for the serendipity of having treated him in a way that left the possibility of this deal open. If I'd have been any number of the other people who hadn't treated him well, the deal would have been dead in the water. You never know who in your life will resurface tomorrow in a role that can advocate for or completely close down the thing you're pitching. When you treat everyone like they might be a decision maker in a future boardroom, you leave yourself open to every opportunity that might present itself.

CHAPTER 11

THE LIE:

IF SHE DOESN'T LOVE ME, I'M NOT LOVABLE

What gives us our sense of confidence? What is it that builds our self-esteem? I used to believe my value was tied directly to the connections I had, the way I looked, or just generally how other people saw me. For way too long, I let the experiences of my past with the opposite sex inform how confident or attractive I felt. I let the way someone liked me, or didn't, influence how likable I believed myself to be.

This bad logic leap was like the faulty thinking of the kid who gets bitten by a dog. *If this dog bites, all dogs must bite.* It's like the person who hears about an airplane crashing and, as a result, has anxiety every time they walk onto a plane, even though the stats say they are more likely to be injured on the car ride over than during takeoff and landing. We do this all the time. We have an experience, and then we let that experience anchor us to the belief that we're likely to repeat that experience. That was the case for me when I first started dating.

Shocker: I was not a prolific dater in the early days. I was an awkward adolescent who didn't consider himself an attractive dating option. My general inability to attract girlfriends, and the later rejection from the few times I did, created something of a complex about who I was and how much I liked myself, let alone loved myself. Now that I'm in my forties, I can see how ridiculous it was to have yielded the power of how I felt about myself to the opinions of other people, but, for whatever reason, when I was in junior high school, high school, and college, I tied my experiences and my feelings together.

Case in point. In those early years of dating I had what, for me, was a pretty serious relationship. Because of the scarcity of getting a yes when I asked someone out, I fell hard and fast once we started dating. That relationship wasn't exactly bringing out the very best in me every day, but it existed, and that in and of itself meant that it needed to be maintained. I was in it because I felt like I was being validated as a person or as a man. I'd twisted the situation into a story I told myself about how someone wanting to be with me and considering me worthy of being loved was the confirmation of my self-worth. Maybe you can relate. I had tied my happiness to the health and welfare of that relationship.

When she was happy with that relationship, I felt happier in my life.

When she wasn't, I wasn't. Classic codependence.

It didn't occur to me that the affirmation I was looking for couldn't actually come from others but had to come from inside myself. That's a lesson you have to live some life to completely grasp. But, in those days, my wants, personal value, and confidence hinged overwhelmingly and unhealthily on the day-to-day status of my relationship.

I'm embarrassed for that version of me.

When we had been dating for about a year, I happened to come by her apartment unannounced. It was late. I wanted to surprise her. I thought it would be cute. I knocked on the door and walked right in like I had so many other times. As I turned the corner in the hallway to her room I heard an unexpected sound. A male voice. When I turned the handle on the door of her room, I already knew what I was about to see.

She was hanging out with another guy.

In bed.

Brutal rug pull.

I was devastated. I went through all the emotions. I started in this unbearably painful period of shock. I couldn't believe this had happened and didn't understand why it had. In a way that made sense then and doesn't now, I needed answers. Over the next week I made a thorough list of all the things I needed to get to the bottom of so I could fully process what I was feeling. In getting my answers, my shock gave way to denial.

"We were just giving each other backrubs, like friends do." She fed me that line and I *actually* believed. I wanted to believe it. I needed to believe it, even though I knew it wasn't true. I want to slap that younger Dave square in the head. Tell him so many things.

My denial gave way to bargaining. This person who had betrayed my trust was now someone I was trying to redraw relationship lines with so we could get on back to neutral.

Bargaining? Completely ineffective in the long term, but it felt like the only way to ease the pain then.

I went through an exhaustive search for what I did wrong that would have led to this. What could I have done to keep this from happening? What could I have changed about myself to preempt the series of events that led to this? What would I need to do in the future to make sure it never happened again?

Of course, it wasn't my fault. I mean I'm sure there were things I could have done to be a better partner then—I was a man-child for goodness sake—but it wasn't a thing that I could have kept from happening necessarily. That recognition completed the cycle of emotions and triggered the dynamic duo of sad and angry. Sangry.

I left the relationship angry for what happened and sad at what it meant for every other relationship I'd enter into going forward. If this dog bites, all dogs must bite. If I have been cheated on, I'll always be cheated on.

It was crushing for my little, immature baby soul. In part, it was an affirmation of all the insecurity I had from years of struggling to keep up with the guys who seemed to get dates like it was no problem. In part, it was one of the first times that I'd made myself a little more vulnerable and, in that vulnerability, was open for the possibility of being hurt on a scale I'd never known before.

What I did not fully appreciate at the time was how seriously this single event would imprint on how I approached relationships from that day forward. My experience now had a new set of evidence: partners cheat because there was something wrong with me, and there was something better in someone else.

For the next few years I entered every relationship with a

suspicion about what might happen if I were to be fully available or totally vulnerable again. On some level, I assumed it was only a matter of time before I would be rejected by the person I was in a relationship with. So, in an attempt to get ahead of that reality, I entered relationships with a fully guarded heart. I created a big defensive barrier around the parts of me that were hurt in that earlier season, which meant I never took the opportunity to be available or fully connect. I sought relationships with women I deemed to have a lower chance of hurting me, and then kept them at arm's length just to be sure.

The interesting revelation all these years later is that I did these things in an attempt to keep myself from being hurt, but by doing the things that were intended to protect me, I was actually guaranteeing that I wouldn't ever have the kind of quality relationship I was interested in. I stopped being myself and instead played a character I thought people needed me to be. Because I'd been myself and was rejected, I kept myself from being authentic or true to who I was inside out of a fear of having another person tell me I wasn't good enough as I am. That inauthenticity and forced distance was a recipe for never truly connecting, for never truly being satisfied. It was complicit in my not being an ideal date for a half decade and, if you read chapter 5 of *Girl, Wash Your Face*, you'll know it nearly cost me my relationship with my now wife and best friend.

When Rachel and I first met, I knew very early on that there was something about her that suggested we were meant to be together. This was paralyzingly frightening because of the experiences I'd had in the past. It seemed rational in my mind to keep her at arm's length so that she wouldn't have the opportunity to hurt me. Of course, that was a recipe for a relationship that was shallow, that lacked meaning and connection on the level it deserved, and that wasn't necessarily something that would inspire someone to want to marry you. In the end, we had to go through a pretty hard season where Rachel finally got sick of my pushing back against being vulnerable and available and said she would never speak to me again. That finally jolted me into realizing that I had to wake up and get out of my own way.

I can see now what I couldn't then: I needed to deconstruct the lies I was believing. I needed to understand that just because I was previously in a bad relationship, it didn't mean that every relationship I would ever have would be bad. And just because I'd once shown my authentic self to someone and was rejected, that did not make me a reject. That early rejection I'd experienced was unique to that situation, to her individual taste, and her taste did not stand as a proxy for all other people, or even any other people. This realization didn't necessarily come easy, but, through hard conversations, some work in therapy, and the benefit of time, I came to see how sad it was to have given away my power to someone who didn't deserve to wield it, the tragedy it was to yield the definition of my self-worth to anyone but myself.

This past fall, Rachel and I threw our first couple's conference called Rise Together. We took the two hundred couples who came together in Austin, Texas, through an exercise where we asked them to describe a negative event that had happened in their relationship. We had them write a word or set of words that represented that event on a rock. It was a physical reminder to stop weaponizing this event in the future version of their relationship, so they could become the people who could get past that thing. Of course, they still needed to go through the work of contrition if apologies were necessary, to commit to therapy if there was still work that needed to be done. But the hope was that, as a couple, they might commit to identifying honestly the things that have acted as barriers, that have gated their relationship and kept it from becoming the very best version of itself.

As they walked those rocks that had been weighing them down to the front of the auditorium and physically dropped them into a trough, it was, as we stood on stage, an absolute miracle to behold.

We watched these couples promise to push into hard conversations about unspoken things that had been limiting their relationships from reaching their fullest potential.

Emotional. Beautiful. Freeing.

The equivalent for each of us, if we're truly interested in connecting with people the way we hope to, is to go through a similar exercise identifying the things we need to stop using as weapons against ourselves. For too many years, I believed that the rejection I experienced in my early twenties was an indication of me being "rejectable." It was an insecure response, an emotional reaction to a series of events that were, in fact, not indicative of my worthiness. As it turned out, they were simply a reflection of one person deciding that I wasn't for her.

The fact that I wasn't for her didn't mean that I wasn't for someone else.

Not being loved by this one person didn't make me unlovable, just as your past heartbreaks don't make you unlovable either.

And someone rejecting you or hurting you doesn't mean that everyone else will.

I see so clearly now what a self-defeating exercise it was to build walls around my heart to keep me from being hurt. Of course, I can also see that something good came out of it—that my being closed off and unavailable for years kept me available long enough for Rachel to grow up, turn nineteen, and meet twenty-seven-year-old, partially broken me. God bless the silver linings. But if I hadn't learned to overcome the lies keeping me from fully connecting, I would have lost her too.

I've learned that if you don't love me—heck, if you don't like me—then I'm not for you. That goes for anything I create, including this book. If you don't like it, or anything else we're producing at the Hollis Company, that just means that it's not for you. I mean, I really can't stand The Lord of the Rings movies. One ring may rule them all—all but me. The fact that I don't like LOTR doesn't make it unlovable. How do I know this? It's one of the biggest film franchises in the universe. It spawned another trilogy called The Hobbit—also something I can't stand—and has done literally billions of dollars in the box office with millions of loyal, loving fans around the world. I'm not one of them, and my not liking it takes nothing away from how lovable it is.

So no matter what you've gone through in your relationship history, don't let the experiences of your past dictate what's available for you in your future. I'm not saying you need to get all Ariana Grande on 'em and say, "Thank U, Next," but carrying the baggage from a past relationship is the equivalent of handing a piece of you to the person who hurt you and asking them to hold on to it while you carry on as only a part of yourself. You, and only you, get to determine your self-worth. The sooner you come to appreciate that you are enough as you are, that you are good as you are, that you are worthy as you are, the sooner you'll be available to connect meaningfully in relationships as your true self.

THINGS THAT HELPED ME

1. **I sat on a stranger's couch.** Therapy is my friend. Therapy is your friend. Sitting with a licensed therapist who could objectively listen to my story and point out the flaws in my logic was invaluable. Getting under the hood of what's led you to who you are and what you believe isn't easy work, but it's incredibly important if you're going to be successful in letting go of things that previously had power over your life.

2. **I took stock of all the people who knew and accepted me as I was.** When you start to believe something negative about yourself, it can be hard to see the evidence that debunks the lies. During the time when I'd convinced myself that I needed to be someone else to attract the right woman, I didn't realize I was showing up every day and being accepted as my authentic self with friends and family and coworkers. This validation of who I was existed in hundreds of moments every single day, but I just hadn't taken the time to take stock of that affirmation. Once I started to appreciate this, it made it easier to believe that the one example where this affirmation didn't exist was the exception and not the rule.

3. **I challenged the voice in my head.** Those sound like the words of a crazy person, but hear this—you get to

decide if you listen to your thoughts or not. You get to challenge the things you think and, even more, push back on why you think the things you do. The decision to not take everything I think at face value allowed me to change the narrative as I, instead, actively considered what was true and what wasn't. If you don't take the time to think about what you think about, you may just believe those thoughts in your head, even the ones that aren't true.

CHAPTER 12

THE LIE:
REAL MEN DON'T SHOW EMOTION

Don't be ridiculous. Of course real men show emotion.

I mean, seriously.

THINGS THAT HELPED ME

1. **I remembered that I'm no longer in seventh grade.** Doing anything—or not doing anything—because of someone else's definition of masculinity feels like peer pressure from grade school. I may have been susceptible to believing I needed a Trapper Keeper if I wanted to be a cool kid back then, but I don't buy into needing to be any way but *my way* as a grown-ass adult. Feeling all the feelings, crying all the tears, admitting when I feel shame or regret or joy or gratitude are things that actually define my human experience, and denying they exist would be denying a huge part of who I am.

2. **I saw the impact that owning emotion can have on business success.** My friend, if you're looking to climb the corporate ladder, attract more customers, or lead your team well, finding ways to use authentic emotion to create empathy with your stakeholders is a game changer. Rachel and I have built a business on authenticity and vulnerability that has propelled our podcasts and books and conferences and products to sell better than we could have ever believed. They sell well because they're grounded in the notion of providing tools to people that can help them change their lives for the better, but it's because they're grounded in showing real emotion that they're effective. As a person who's operating a multimillion-dollar company that has dozens and dozens of employees and their families depending on our continued success, the willingness to tap into and show our emotions is a big part of how we'll continue to grow.

3. **I saw the importance of modeling my emotions to my children.** As a parent, I want to make sure that my boys grow up knowing that feeling things is the way we know we're alive. When we went through our season with foster care and adoption, I let my boys see my tears so they could appreciate the importance of sadness. When we achieve a new goal as a family or as a business, we make sure our children are a part of the celebration so they appreciate the importance of feeling achievement. In a world where technology makes it harder and harder to connect, modeling comfort in expressing emotion, and therefore helping them feel comfortable expressing emotion, is part of how I can gauge what's happening in their lives, particularly as they move into the teen years.

CHAPTER 13

THE LIE:

I KNOW WHAT SHE NEEDS

When Rachel was on the back end of a fifty-two-hour labor with our first son and the doctor came in and told her it was finally time to push, I did what I knew she needed most. I pulled up Trick Daddy's "Let's Go" and turned it up. Way up. I thought the contagious beat and the melodic perfection that comes from adding in Twista and Lil Jon were precisely what that moment called for.

Incorrect. That was not my greatest choice. It turned out Rachel, in fact, did not need that song to help her bring our cherub into the world. She definitely didn't need it on volume level eight.

I'm going to lead with the conclusion of this chapter first: If you're in a relationship and you have a preconception that you know what your partner is going to need from you in the future, you're wrong. If you thought you knew what your partner needed before you were in a relationship, before you got under the hood and really understood their wiring and how yours and theirs shake hands, again, you've set yourself up for disappointment.

If you are anything like me, your idea of how you should treat a partner was influenced by some combination of your parents' views, societal norms in your formative years, the example of your closest friends, and depictions of how relationships worked on television and in movies. All of these things, as well intended as they may have been, are missing two critical ingredients:

1. Knowing how *your* partner is specifically wired—from the unique nuances of their personality and their communication style to the way they give and receive love.
2. The flexibility to change as life changes—your vision of what your partner needs cannot be a static snapshot but a motion picture that moves as the stories and stages of your life develop (we'll get to that more in the next chapter).

It's laughable now to look back at the beginning of our relationship and think I had any concept of what Rachel needed. The hubris in assuming I knew was one thing. The pride that made me cling to what I believed for fear it would reveal how little I knew was another thing, and it kept us from connecting on a deeper level for far too long. So, let me save you some time: if you want an exceptional relationship, you better humble yourself to the possibility that you don't know anything about what your partner needs until you do some work. Stay connected to the reality that the things they needed yesterday will be different from what they need today and what they'll need tomorrow.

Now, even though what your partner needs is different from what mine needs or even what your partner will need in another season of life, I do think you can learn to use some foundational tools that will unbelievably increase the chances of your showing up the way they will need you to, regardless of what that turns out to be. And yes—I once made fun of people who tried to convince me that hooey like this was real and made a difference. But I moved past my limiting beliefs about the science of how we're wired or how we love, and I gave it a try . . . and in doing so have been blown away by the power of what this understanding arms you with in a relationship.

My first recommendation: push aside any bias you may have with the notion of "personality tests" and do a little research on what they are and how they may help you better understand how you're built, how your partner is built, and how your differences come together, both the strengths and weaknesses. In our premarital work, Rachel and I did something called the Myers–Briggs test, a diagnostic that tries to lay out how you make decisions or see the world. In various work environments, I've used something called a DISC test, a tool that sorts possible hires into four personality types—Dominance, Influence, Steadiness, and Conscientiousness—in an attempt to better understand how this new human puzzle piece you're considering fits into your bigger team puzzle.

There's Big Five, EQSQ, 16PF, and about a hundred other tests that, if I wrote them all out, would read more like the census chapters in the book of Numbers, but the point is, these tools are there to help you interact better with the people who matter in your life. These tools take the mystery away from how someone is wired and allow you, with this set of information, to approach your partner in a way they can better receive your approach.

My wife and I in recent years have become huge fans of two tools that have fundamentally transformed how we're able to connect with each other: the Enneagram and love languages. The first helps us better appreciate our personalities and how they work together, and the second helps us understand the different ways we give and receive love.

Hello.

Are you still with me?

Is this thing still on?

Look, maybe you're totally comfortable with this, but I can admit that I struggled not to feel a little weird about spending time understanding these things better. The idea that a man might have to do some work to actually understand how a woman he wants to marry is wired felt like it implied an ineptness that I didn't want to admit. Maybe I hadn't done the work during dating? Was I on the outside of knowledge that better, more evolved men knew like the back of their hand? Also, for some reason, as a person who was raised in a Christian household, there was something even more taboo about turning to science to understand how humans work.

Bottom line, I'm telling you: if you can push past the eye-rolling stigma about tools like these, they will change your life and your relationship. And, if it's what you're hoping for, knowing your partner better and connecting with them on a level that appreciates where they're coming from and meeting them there will lead to one thing for sure: you'll definitely make out more.

Let's start with the Enneagram. This personality diagnostic breaks each of us into one of nine different types. We had *The Sacred Enneagram* author Christopher Heuertz on our *Rise Together* podcast, and he explained that all of us fall into one of the following categories:

Type 1: Perfectionist: those who are principle-based, responsible, and idealize goodness in all things.

Type 2: Giver: people who are self-sacrificing, genuinely kind, and incredibly nurturing.

Type 3: Achiever: the kind of folks who add value to everything they participate in, driven, and ambitious.

Type 4: Romantic: the most emotionally attended of all the types, sees beauty in everything, and draws significance out of all they touch.

Type 5: Observer: lifelong learners who can evaluate, analyze, and figure out solutions to almost any problem.

Type 6: Skeptic: the best contingency planners, threat forecasters, and team players who seek to bring stability to their relationships.

Type 7: Enthusiast: the most curious and imaginative of all the types, forever young, playful, but also the fastest thinkers.

Type 8: Protector: true advocates of the oppressed and vulnerable, present as contrarians, and absolutely tenacious but not as tough as they come across.

Type 9: Peacemaker: natural arbitrators and mediators, these folks maintain inner peace and balance by harmonizing their worlds.[1]

Unless you're a cyborg, you fall into one of these categories. You have one of these as a primary personality trait and one of these as a secondary trait. There are some further interesting details on how each of these types acts when they're sure of themselves versus when they're stressed, and how their virtues and vices manifest. But for Rachel and my relationship, and I'll argue for yours, the most powerful tool that came from this exercise was understanding how these different types pair with others.

I'm a 9, a peacemaker. My wife is a 3, an achiever. Reading the description of how a 9 and a 3 pair is like reading an excerpt from my diary. To be clear, I don't have a diary because, while it may not seem like it, there are certain lines that even I will not cross for this book, but if I did . . .

The Enneagram Institute is one of many organizations that provide insight for free on the dang internet. I learned so much about my relationship straight from their site, and the detail about how Rachel and I pair was so spot on that I was worried someone from some secret Enneagram society was living in our house unannounced and wrote these insights from observing our relationship specifically. *Get out from under our bed, Stuart, and take the tape recorder with you.* It's uncanny. It's so accurate. It's an answer key to the opportunities and pitfalls of our relationship, and it exists on the internet as a resource for you, for free, today.

Yes, we've read books, interviewed that expert on our podcast, and spent more time than most getting deeper into what the Enneagram means and how to use it, but it's a resource that's there for the taking if you're just willing to do a little work. Details about your pairing are available if you want them, and it will blow your mind how closely it aligns with the words you write in your diary, real or imagined.

But wait, there's more. In our relationship, the personality piece was where it started. The notion of love languages was the next step, and a game changer. I know. You may be bristling at the thought, because you're too cool for something called love languages. Listen here, Mr. T, just like an old episode of *The A-Team*, we're getting you on this plane one way or another. You can be cool, or you can connect on a level that leads to make-outs on the regular and a feeling of being loved and seen in your relationship forever.

Even though we had been introduced to his books years earlier, in 2019 we had the opportunity to interview another dream guest for our *Rise Together* podcast: Dr. Gary Chapman, the author of dozens and dozens of relationship books, including *The 5 Love Languages*, which at the time had sold more than 12 million copies and lived for five years running on the *New York Times* best seller list since it released in the US. The idea behind the book is simple, and for those who lean into and apply the learning to their lives, it can be transformational.

For more than forty-five years, Dr. Chapman has been on staff at the same church in Winston-Salem, North Carolina, sometimes as a pastor, always as a marriage and family therapist. For decades, men and women would start counseling sessions with him explaining that they felt like their spouse didn't love them anymore, and that led to him trying to find the patterns in what he was hearing. Sure enough, he went back through years of notes, and every time someone in his office said their partner didn't love them, he asked what it was they were saying they needed. Those needs fell into five categories, which would become the five love languages. We all have one of these as the primary way we need to receive love. If we want our partners to feel love, we have to express it in their language. From our conversation with Dr. Chapman, the love languages are:

1. **Words of affirmation**—using words to build up the other person. "You look so pretty in that color blue."
2. **Gifts**—a gift says, "He was thinking about me. Look what he got for me." (And it's not about the cost of the gift—in this instance it's truly the thought that counts.)
3. **Acts of service**—doing something for your spouse that you know they would like. Cooking a meal, washing dishes, and vacuuming floors are all acts of service.
4. **Quality time**—by which I mean giving your spouse your undivided attention. Taking a walk together or sitting on the couch with the TV off—talking and listening.
5. **Physical touch**—holding hands, hugging, kissing, getting busy in the bedroom, are all expressions of love.[2]

The overwhelming majority of couples have *different* love languages. We're attracted to people who are different from us, and understanding the way each of us in a relationship needs to receive love will be instructive for how we give love. I'm a person who responds most to "acts of service," meaning, if my wife wants me to feel love, the thing she could do first is some small act that in my eyes stands as the literal manifestation of her love. Because I look to receive love in that way, at the beginning of our relationship, it was also the way I would show my love. *If I need love this way, doesn't everyone?* Of course, it couldn't be further from the truth. I just didn't know it. Rachel is a person who's wired for "words of affirmation," which made it hard for me to understand why she didn't respond as I hoped after I'd perform an act of service for her in an attempt to show my love.

"Look, babe, I brought you coffee, and I went to Target and picked up all the things on your shopping list." Her response was, "Thanks." Not like a shrew, but also not in a way that suggested I'd hit the mark on making sure she knew I'd done it because I loved her. She doesn't receive love the way I do. Instead, she was looking for me to acknowledge her hard work, the way she looked, the effort she'd made with whatever was happening in our lives *with my words*. She's wired that way, and when I didn't know it, I kept trying to deliver my showcase of love for her in a way that suited me but not her. Once we understood all this, we showed love in totally different ways, connecting according to how we each were made.

The same goes for you and your most important relationships. If you don't know how they need to receive love, you'll consistently miss the mark, feel frustrated for failing to deliver what you intended, and more than likely leave this person you care about feeling that same frustration for not having felt the love themselves. Finding out what love language you each speak is like getting an answer key for your relationship. Not using it, especially when it's a free resource, is choosing to stay in your own way. Stop it.

While we're on the topic, there are tons of books from Dr. Chapman about relationships, but the other mind-blower for us was his book *When Sorry Isn't Enough* that he cowrote with Jennifer Thomas. In our conversation, Dr. Chapman explained that "in the same way couples miss each other in their efforts to love, they also miss each other in their efforts to apologize." This book uses much of the same methodology and is based on a similar basic principle as the love languages, but it acknowledges that there are unique ways each of us needs to hear "sorry." In their research, Chapman and Thomas asked thousands of people two questions: (1) When you apologize, what are the typical things you say or do? (2) When someone's apologizing to you, what are you looking for them to say? The answers fell into five categories that would become the five languages of apology, as he explained on our podcast:

- **Expressing regret**—actually using words to express that you're sorry with the inclusion of what it is that you're sorry for. Conveying, "I feel bad about what I've done."
- **Accepting responsibility**—expressing that you were wrong, should not have done that, that there is no excuse for the way you behaved. Conveying, "I accept responsibility."
- **Making restitution**—Finding a way to make the wrong right. Conveying, "What can I do to make it right?"
- **Genuinely repenting**—Expressing the desire to change the behavior. Conveying, "I don't like what I did, and I don't want to keep doing it. Can you help me make a plan?"
- **Requesting forgiveness**—Asking the person wronged if they can find it in themselves to forgive you. Conveying, "I value our relationship, I know I've hurt you, will you forgive me?"

To be clear, this is not an ad. Sure, I think you should read both books to really understand what is just the tip of an iceberg here, but for both *The 5 Love Languages* and *When Sorry Isn't Enough*, I get nothing out of my advocacy but the satisfaction of your finding a way to better connect with your partner. The same goes for any assistance you might find with the Enneagram. These are simply tools that have had a massive impact on Rachel's and my pursuit of an exceptional relationship.

Pushing past the lie fueled by my hubris that I didn't need tools to understand how my partner needed me allowed me to show love in an unbelievably better way. Consistently. Our willingness to understand the science in how we're wired took love and intimacy to higher levels and has acted as a shortcut through arguments, and a vehicle to avoiding them altogether in many instances.

THINGS THAT HELPED ME

1. **I took the taboo out of the tools.** Any of the negativity I associated with reaching for and using relationship tools was quickly erased by their power to help drive my relationship forward and help it evolve into something bigger, faster. A younger version of myself would see looking to things like the Enneagram and love languages, to podcasts and books, as something only for people who were broken, inexperienced, uncool, or somehow less of a man. But, having been the beneficiary of the fruit that's come from these resources, I now see my former self as foolish and prideful at the expense of being full. Push your preconceived notions of what it means to take help, and embrace the answer keys that exist, often for free, as the route to the more exceptional version of your relationship.

2. **I committed to putting in the work of relationship development.** Having an exceptional relationship will not happen without work. Our decision to go to therapy and sign up for personal-development conferences, and the way that we push each other to read a new book or listen to a new podcast, are reflections of our intention. If you want to be a better bowler, you have to hit the lanes on the regular. You want to be a better hunter? You have to learn how to stalk and hunt (frankly, I have no idea what you have to do to be a better hunter, because I only just moved to Texas, so that's not my jam . . . yet). The bottom line: when we have things in our lives that we want to get better at, we know it will take work and time to get closer to our goals. It's not often we think about our relationships that way, and it's time we deconstructed any barriers that would keep us from the kind of relationship we want and deserve.

3. **I filtered other people's relational feedback based on their track records.** Have you ever been in a situation where the person giving you relationship advice couldn't themselves hold one down? In the same way I wouldn't come to someone who was totally out of shape for advice on working out, the idea of giving weight to the opinions of someone who isn't excelling in their relationship is ridiculous. Plenty of people have tried to tell us the best way Rachel and I should be doing our marriage. If those voices come from people who are killing it in their own relationship, their thoughts are welcome. But . . . if the feedback you're getting is coming from someone who can't keep a steady relationship, you best filter out their feedback as it does not come from a credible source.

CHAPTER 14

THE LIE:

MY ROLE IN THIS RELATIONSHIP IS CONSTANT

If you find yourself thinking you'll succeed in your relationship by holding tight to the role you currently play, the identity you presently carry, or the version of how you show up today for the balance of your relationship, you're either wrong or destined to be done with this relationship sooner than you'd like.

Tools like those from the last chapter were only half the battle. Knowing how our personalities paired and how Rachel needed love or apologies was critical if I was going to meet her where she needed to be met. The next layer would reveal itself over time: the *identity* I needed to play for her during the different seasons of our life together. Who did she need me to be in the broader sense as a partner? I came into our marriage thinking identity was a fixed thing that would stay the same throughout our relationship. I could not have been more wrong.

In business, there are plenty of examples of thought leaders reminding us to continually consider how we need to *evolve this business or die*. That, if we hold to what worked for business generally or this business specifically in the past, without staying attuned to how the customer changes, technology changes, or the culture changes, we just won't keep up with consumer needs and have a product that's as relevant or as easy to compel the consumer to buy.

So why are we less open to the kind of changes we might need to implement in our own personal relationships to stay relevant with the needs of our partners, our family, and our friends? Openness to the necessity of change in business is seen as a core value. Openness to the necessity of change in a relationship, though, was something I took as an indictment of me. When presented with the need for change, I saw it as an implication that I was in some way failing to live up to my end of the bargain. It felt personal in a way the business example didn't.

But the truth is, as you mature as individuals and as a couple, and as life introduces new stages, those unique stages create differences in who you are and how you approach things. Those new stages will also force you to take on a new identity for this person you're in relationship with if you intend to love them well. And that's okay. That's more than okay. I don't mean you should change who you are at your core or sacrifice what it means to be you, but you can bring who you are to your partner in different ways according to what they need during a particular week, month, or year. Those who are able to identify the needs of their partner from stage to stage and adjust to meet those needs are the ones who will build the strongest relationships. This adaptiveness will not only act as a catalyst to drive the relationship further in good times, but it will also create a bond that allows you to weather the storms that inevitably come.

Who I need to be for Rachel has changed in just about every stage of life in a way that's totally disconnected from what I thought it was going to be like when we were first dating or married. It's healthy to learn to expect this and to accept that, in the maturation of your partnership, you'll need to be present in different ways along that journey.

To pursue this proactively, you can start by asking your partner a simple question: "How do you think I can best show up in your life?"

Talking together about what needs exist in this season, in this month, will inform how you take the best of you and bring it for the best of your relationship. Even asking the question is going to score you points for wanting to try. Swallowing your ego and admitting that you don't always have the self-awareness to know if what you're doing is best serving them, best serving the relationship? Well, that's a master-level move.

More than anything, hear this: it's not rocket science, but getting to the bottom of what your loved one needs from you as a partner, just to see if what they say they need aligns with what you believe they need, could be the difference between your being in a good relationship or an exceptional one.

There are plenty of examples from my relationship with Rachel that, when I look back now, make me think, *How silly of me to think what she needed was . . .* Over and over, my thinking I knew what she wanted usually came at the expense of giving her what would have benefited her most. If I had just been thoughtful enough to have a conversation about what kind of me she needed in order to tackle the events on that day, I would have been able to actually be present in a way that brought out the very best in her and our marriage.

Back at the very, very beginning of our marriage, I thought so differently than I do now about who Rachel was and how I should be a partner for her. Rachel and I first dated when I was twenty-six years old and she was eighteen going on twenty-nine. She was a baby. She was a small baby rabbit. I was the scene from *Swingers*, afraid that I might shred her to pieces with my bear claws. Was it *Swingers*? Was it *Of Mice and Men*? Somewhere there is a story about a bear that has a small rabbit in its clutches, and the baby rabbit dies. I came into our relationship with this worldly "I've lived more years than you"-ness that, when combined with my more traditional upbringing in a house where my father worked and my mother stayed home, had me presupposing some of the roles—gender roles, relational roles—that each of us should play. As for how I played the role of the man in the relationship, I thought it was my job to take care of this woman.

To be clear, I hope you *do* have the compulsion to take care of the person you are in relationship with, but the problem in my thinking was the implication that she could not take care of herself. I know so very clearly now that Rachel Hollis—trust me, every day of the week and twice on Sundays—can take care of herself. I know that now and wish I'd known it then, but at that time, I felt I had a handle on the way the world worked and I thought my job was to take care of her.

A major part of that was financial.

I'd been working for a longer period of time and was making more money than she was at that point, so I saw my role as the provider. The unspoken, darker side to my thinking, whether it was conscious or unconscious, was the assumption that since I made more money I had permission to not be engaged in the things that were required to make a house a home.

My expectations at the beginning of our marriage made more sense to my parents than they truly did to me. If you don't have a conversation about who's going to do the cooking or the cleaning, or what it means for one person in the relationship to make more money, and whether making more money somehow absolves you of doing chores around the house or lets you off the hook from having to cook dinners, I promise that's a recipe for a lot of friction in your relationship.

I can see in retrospect that my assumption that Rachel just needed me to be the provider was simply wrong. What she needed at the beginning of our marriage was for me to approach it as a partnership where we openly and honestly had conversations about who was going to do what as we shared the load of this life we were starting together.

Guess what? I was young and dumb and had to learn this the hard way.

A few years into being married, we had kids. Though I was supportive during Rachel's pregnancy, sympathizing with its impact on her changing body and emotions to the best of my ability, it was hard for me when the baby finally arrived. I wasn't sure what I was supposed to do. Some things inherently came along with motherhood that bonded my wife with our son. The baby had grown inside her body and was fed by her body, so I struggled to find my place, my sense of connection. Their bond reinforced my belief that my primary role was simply to provide for their sustenance.

My response after the first couple of weeks was, "Hey, I've got to get back to work. So I need to make sure I can get a little bit more sleep." What I didn't say but implied was, "I need to get more sleep than you because my job requires me to be awake in a way that your job doesn't." To be clear, Rachel's job while she was on maternity leave was taking care of a human being whose life depended on her being awake enough to care for him. The only reason I have a twelve-year-old today is that she was able to keep him alive when I went to work. Back then, though, I rationalized wanting to sleep on a couch away from the baby with the money that might come from doing better at my job, and I gave earning money more value than Rachel sleeping enough to care for our first son.

That value assessment doesn't make sense to me today. I wish I could go back in a time machine and be a little more understanding, and certainly in a way where it was not all about my beauty rest. Goodness gracious.

As we've built our careers, I think of myself (and I think she'd agree) as Rachel's number one cheerleader. I am just wildly, massively, ridiculously proud of the work she's done and continues to do. But I am also the practical, pragmatic person who has historically been more grounded, not wanting to let too much of a dream, too big of a dream, too audacious of a dream get ahold of her. That way, if she ended up not being able to attain that dream for whatever reason, she wouldn't find herself disappointed (see the finale of our documentary *Rachel Hollis Presents: Made for More* on Amazon). I am an expectations manager. It's in my DNA.

When we'd had our two oldest kids, Rachel's momentum with her business really started growing. Even some ten years ago, she already had a clear vision for where this all was going. But me? I thought it was neat to have this daring sense of what was possible for the future, but I truly thought my role was to be a supportive listener, and of course to cheer for her, but just not too much. My job was to temper some of what she thought was possible so she wouldn't be disappointed if it didn't come together.

I promise, it came from a place of love.

I really, truly believed that what she needed most from me, as the practical person in our relationship, was pragmatism. If I could, I'd try to convince my younger self that there's a version of this that still stays true to its valuable pragmatic roots but that comes alongside and believes in the dream of the dreamer without minimizing it, without trying to manage expectations around it.

One time, when Rachel told me about a very ambitious dream of taking her career to the next level with a potential deal, I thought, *You're crazy, and my job in this season is to keep you from thinking you can actually do this because I love you so much I want to protect you from disappointment.* What I actually said to her was, "Come on, babe, there's like a million-to-one chance of that happening."

She was incredulous.

"A million-to-one chance?" she demanded. "They've already asked for follow-up meetings."

Okay, that was true, and I had to give it to her—at the very least to get the look off her face.

"Okay then, maybe not a million to one but, like, a 3 percent chance that this will actually happen."

Yeah, that didn't sit well with her.

Though it came from a place of love, it was received in a way that contradicted my intent. What I was saying was "I don't want you to be disappointed," but in part I was also saying, "I don't believe you can do this." In fact, I gave her a 97 percent chance that she wouldn't.

When I really sit with it, I realize I was also saying, "I don't think you're strong enough to deal with the consequences of trying but not achieving your dream," which makes me want to cry a little bit more. What a brutal realization. My attempt to play my role well and to keep my wife from being disappointed signaled over and over that I either didn't think she was capable or didn't think she was strong enough to deal with adversity.

Rachel knew what she was doing. She knew this vision she had. I assumed a role of trying to keep her from getting ahead of herself, from getting excited and then being let down. *I was misguided.*

About six months later, I came home from work to find a box on the table.

"What is this?" I asked.

"It's a gift you got me," she said.

"Oh my goodness, I'm so glad I got it for you. What did I get you?"

I handed her the box, and she opened it. Inside was a little charm on a bracelet. And that little charm had "3%" stamped on it. That thing she'd told me she was going to do, the one I'd told her there was a 3 percent chance of her doing? She had gotten confirmation that day that the network wanted to sign her on contract. She would be the host of a nationally syndicated cable television program. She would do that thing that I'd given her next to no chance of achieving.

"I got this as a reminder that even my best friend and biggest supporter occasionally only gives me a 3 percent chance of accomplishing my dreams, and I can't let that keep me from trying. If I had listened to you, I wouldn't have kept trying." She wore that bracelet around her wrist every day for years as she built our company.

Now that's a master class in effective passive aggression.

And thank God for that. I thank God that I, in my attempt to be who I thought she needed, didn't talk her out of doing the things she knew she was on this planet to do. I'm so grateful that she, in that case and basically any case when it comes to dreams, didn't listen to my pragmatic self, regardless of how well-intentioned I may have been.

Every instance I think back on where I didn't support her in the way she needed has turned into a learning experience that helps me support her better in the future. When you stop to think about it, I know you'll also find times when you presented with best intentions but showed up in a way that didn't optimally serve your relationship too.

Beyond learning how to be a better supporter, when you've been in a relationship for a long enough period of time, you'll also learn that sometimes one of you will be the lead horse and other times it will fall on your partner. Taking turns being the strongest doesn't make you weak; it makes you human. Rachel and I have taken turns embodying the identity of being the person who is the stronger of the two of us over and over in our marriage, trading off whose primary job it is to be stronger for the other.

This back-and-forth happened during our adoption journey, where she drove the start of our journey and I took the baton at the low point and pushed us home. It had me stepping up as she worked through struggles with anxiety, and it saw her leading out as I tripped over that bridge from my thirties to forties. Every couple of years, life has dealt us something that required an adjustment in how we support each other.

We've traded off holding up mirrors for each other even when we didn't want to have the conversation. We've alternated as each other's motivational speaker when we struggled with the shame of not being what each other or the kids deserved.

Fluidly taking on that mantle of leadership when one of us most needed it took us to where we are today. She cast a vision for what working together could look like, helped me create the leverage I needed to leave my job, and led us to move to Austin. I cooked up the plans for the "what" and "how" questions, dug into the details of how to get an operation up and running, and got knee deep in all the nitty-gritty. Sitting here at the end of an absolutely incredible year, I can see clearly that so many of these things happened in part because of a role exchange between partners. It took a lot of work and a really hard string of conversations, but this willingness to take turns leading our relationship by leaning into our individual strengths produced the success that we're experiencing today.

It's also meant that, identity-wise in our relationship, my role has changed yet again as I shed what it was for me to be a person who worked in the traditional entertainment industry to be one who now works with Rachel. I've gone from a person giving direction to a team around the world to being in a business partnership with my spouse that requires a very collaborative approach (an intentionally nuanced one if you want to still feel like making out after a long day at the office). In real time, it's been an incredible challenge from an ego perspective for both of us to try to work well together and, frankly, for me to learn to let go of some of the shallow stuff that came with the status and access of my old job where I was more in the spotlight.

Yes, I have the opportunity now to lead this incredible team of ours with a mission to equip people to change themselves and change the world. It's exciting. But it also requires me to become comfortable leading a team where our creative visionary and the face of the business is not me. Our company's life force, my wife, is spectacularly amazing and, at the same time, vainly, is not me.

And thank goodness for that. I'm clearheaded enough to appreciate that the amazing things we're creating come largely as a product of her vision, of her listening to the audience and trying to create tools that can answer the needs of this community. My role is to step in as the leader of this organization. It is about creating order around *her* organization that she spent a decade and a half of sweat equity building so we can do bigger work, better work, work that reaches more people as it becomes *our* company.

I'll finish this chapter with one more suggestion: challenge yourself to think about what *you* need as well. What do you need in this relationship that you currently are not getting because of the way the other person is supporting you (or not supporting you)? Can you represent those needs in a way that the person can hear it and not get defensive? That's the challenge of challenges. But when you get to that place, when you can ask your partner what they need and also find a way to represent your needs that are not being met, that's when you can take the relationship to the next level.

I am going now to ask Rachel what she needs and how I can

best meet those needs. By asking, I'm hoping I might be a little more deliberate in delivering those things to her while helping us find even more of the alignment that fuels our relationship. I hope you'll do the same.

THINGS THAT HELPED ME

1. **I employed "radical candor."** Through the years, I've taken my teams through a conversation about the benefit of resolving issues in real time. Kim Scott wrote an entire book about this concept (that also has a fantastic twenty-minute YouTube video of her explaining it), but the bottom line is that there is a way to both challenge someone directly and care about them personally at the same time.[1] In fact, the main thing I took away is that if you care about someone, finding a way to give them feedback that would help them or your relationship is the key to cutting something off before it becomes a bigger issue that's harder to solve. Rachel and I dive into conflict in a constructive way on a daily basis. It may be uncomfortable at times, but dealing with small discomfort to get on the same page is wildly better than letting things fester, create resentment, or become issues that are harder to defuse.

2. **I continue to come back to what's best for our relationship.** So much of what we learn about how we're *supposed* to be in a relationship comes out of the experiences of other people. We model ourselves after people who are living their lives, not ours. Those people, that societal norm, the opinions of my friends who do their

relationships differently than I do? They aren't in this relationship. I am. We are. What works for us is right, because it works for us, even if it doesn't make sense or work as well for others. We have to consistently resist the trap of comparing what we have with what others have. We have to take their advice, their passive aggression, their side-eyed disapproval for what it's worth. Again, if they're killing it in their relationship, give their advice more time as you consider if there's something practically applicable for yours. If they aren't killing it in their relationship or have views that contradict what you believe, pay them no attention. They aren't in your relationship. You are. Together. Keep coming back to what serves you best.

3. **I started checking in on my relationship regularly.** When you approach your relationship with the kind of intention you'll need to take it to the next level, you'll start asking if your calendar reflects the way you want to be present. You'll ask if you've taken a pause from your regularly scheduled programming to check and see if the way you're supporting your partner is actually what is needed. Set a reminder in your calendar to touch base with your partner and confirm that you're on the same page. This is something Rachel and I do every Sunday night. The possibility of one of us making a wrong assumption about the other is wildly reduced because of our habit of asking better questions regularly.

CHAPTER 15

THE LIE:

IF THEY DON'T NEED ME, THEY WON'T WANT ME

Speaking of identity shifts, as I mentioned, *I used to be the breadwinner of our family.*

Then I left my job.

As my wife's career took off and had her earning more than I ever had.

By a stretch.

We'd never spent time talking about the role either of us played in contributing to the family, and certainly it wasn't the cornerstone of our relationship. Nonetheless, that shift was jarring for me.

I mean, I obviously love that she's had success; but in a way that I couldn't have predicted, her success did something to a central role I'd played for so many years in our marriage that it acted as an insecurity trigger I didn't see coming.

Rachel's books have worked, and her live events have worked, and in those most insecure moments, I asked this question: My identity has in part been grounded in her need for me and the provision that comes from my salary—now that she is the primary earner for our family, *now that she doesn't need me, will she still want me*?

Yo.

Now, this chapter isn't about working or not, earning more or less. This is about the logic traps we fall into about our values in a relationship. The kind of contingencies we put on why they're with us in the first place. How those assumptions are tested when life changes, expectedly or unexpectedly.

It's not *if* but *when*: you will find a role you've played in the past upended. Good and bad. Promotions and unexpected sickness. You may not identify with a shift in the role of breadwinner, but I'll argue that role shifts can arrive with a diagnosis, deployment, emerging business, evolving life stage, or the stay-at-home parent who's taken on the hardest job in the world but is now faced with a similar set of questions as kids leave the nest.

The wild thing about this question is that it's not just something I struggle with when it comes to Rachel. I've operated in a surprisingly transactional mindset in all kinds of relationships over my lifetime. I've taken some philosophies about exerting leverage in a business deal to convince the other party to reciprocate and applied that same logic to my own personal relationships.

In so many ways, that transactional mindset is built on a foundation of insecurity and fear. A lot of it goes back to experiences I had when I was growing up where, for whatever reasons, I didn't have the most confidence. This fostered a worry that people might only love me back if they needed something I could tangibly provide in relationship as a *gift with purchase*. Not a healthy way to think. I get it. Beyond that, the obligation I felt to continue to provide whatever that thing was became exhausting.

Inevitably, when I finally did receive proof that I was in fact not *needed* in any relationship, I began to question if I was still *wanted*. Gulp.

This was the case with my wife. For the majority of our relationship, my wife was an entrepreneur. She's still an entrepreneur, but when we met, she was working in a conventional and traditional job setting in the movie industry. I needed to get creative approvals from her boss for things like movie posters, which required that I go through her. What started very professionally devolved very quickly, and we went from being colleagues who were working together to humans who were starting a life together.

Not long after we were married, as I'd progressed a bit in my career, Rachel decided that the conventional work environments she'd worked in weren't for her. She went from Miramax to an advertising agency. From an ad agency to a production company. Then her passion called her to create something of her own. She was excited about the opportunity to launch something in an entrepreneurial fashion, and I was happy about the opportunity to support her in this launch.

At this time, I was the one with the reliable paycheck. I was the one who could be counted on in the ups and downs of her trying to do something that would most certainly work, but that didn't have as certain a timetable. I wasn't making a wild amount of money when she made this pivot, but when she was thinking about the kind of capital that might be required to start her business, it was my paycheck that took care of us as a couple and ultimately our family when we started creating humans.

I was needed most then and, therefore, in my mind, loved most then.

Ridiculous.

Only in the last year or so have I come to fully appreciate how I associated Rachel's ability to take more risks during the building of her company with the stability my paycheck offered in those early days. That concept of being a backstop, and all the warped transactional qualities it came with in my mind, made me more secure about our love back then.

If I'm honest, I hadn't thought the identity I took on as a "provider" could be a bad thing . . . until she created so much value in what she'd built that my financial contributions were no longer a part of the backstop equation. For the better part of a decade, even though she'd built a thriving, growing business, I'd taken some satisfaction in knowing that she needed me and my salary as a safety net every time she went to expand.

Then my wife outgrew that need.

I found myself reverting to some of the insecurities from my dating days.

The suggestion that she was with me for what I could provide for her financially was, frankly, in retrospect, insulting. There never was a time when she decided to be with me because of what my job might afford in security, connections, access, or anything else. It was quite the opposite.

If you find yourself, like I did, connecting your partner's love with some material thing, some role you play, identity you assume, or some attribute you have (that over time may transition or dwindle), you really have to ask some deeper and bigger questions about the foundation of your relationship. Because you're either believing this lie and buying into the insecurities that come with it, or you're in a bad relationship where your partner is in it for the wrong reasons.

If you're in a relationship that only values what you can give, is that the kind of relationship you really want to be in? And if it's not that, can you see how thinking that someone is only in it for what they can get out of you doesn't serve you or your relationship? That this mindset may hold you back from a deeper relationship?

As I said, this wasn't just a mistake I made with Rachel. I made this same mistake many times in my friendships, trying to game the system and manufacture scenarios where people I was hoping to be friends with would want to be friends with me. But gaming a system to get people to like you? So not necessary. I was thinking that if I could provide people with things, or access, or both, then they would want to be in relationship with me. They'd like those free movie passes or my ability to walk them into Disneyland. But the fact that a movie premiere could come as a gift with purchase in our friendship had me always second-guessing if my friendships were real, or a means to an end. Blargh.

Especially in the past five years, I've struggled to find meaningful friendships with other guys, and in that struggle I've made decisions that did me no good. It makes me sad now to think about how little faith I had in myself that I felt I had to construct such elaborate schemes to put a finger on the scale in my favor. Instead of building friendships based on connection and shared interest, I was trying to convince these folks I was worthy of their friendship.

Of course, I can see now that the tilting of the game didn't actually give me a chance at the friendships I hoped for over the twenty-five years I worked in entertainment. After entering into community with these normal humans and establishing the rules that governed our relationships with some of the perks from a world they thought was cool, I grew resentful of the implication that giving out my log-on for some subscription account or inviting someone as my plus-one to the next corporate event was the only reason they would be friends with me. My transactional brain ruined any chance for my emotional heart.

I wasn't mindful of these unintended consequences until it was too late. I compromised friendships that should not have been compromised, and that wouldn't have been if not for my own insecurity. I know now that I can't have any relationship that will matter if the other person doesn't want to be in it for me rather than what I can bring. You may be uniquely skilled in some capacity, and as much as your friends or partner can be the grateful recipients of that thing you alone bring, if your relationships hinge on those other things and not just you and who you are, they don't mean anything and will leave you feeling sad, resentful, or both.

Whether it's a friendship or a romantic relationship, a connection based on *need* and not *want* isn't a real relationship. Contingent love isn't real love. Yes, you and I each offer something unique, but we need to be careful that the unique something is who we are and not some version of who we think others want us to be or some material thing that might cause us to question their motives.

Yes, this beautiful woman Rachel and I need each other, but we aren't with each other because of that need, or even the things we can do for each other. We're with each other because of our want, and appreciating that difference has made all the difference.

THINGS THAT HELPED ME

1. **I pushed back against the temptation to sweeten the pot.** We just aren't friends with people who need things from us as a condition of our friendship. That seems so obvious, but it's taken time for me to get there. If you find yourself in relationships individually or as a couple where you're always the one expected to pay, drive, coordinate sitters, go to their choice of restaurant, or whatever it may be, you need to push to a place where there's parity in the relationship, or you'll come to resent it.

2. **I performed "scream tests."** In every job I've ever had we produced a ridiculous amount of reports. Every year, I'd stop sending them to their usual distribution list to see who screamed, to see who actually noticed that they were gone. If you're in a relationship that feels unbalanced, where it feels like you're having to bring something beyond yourself as a condition of the relationship, pull that thing back and see what happens. If you get a "scream," it will tee you up for a great (maybe hard) conversation. If you don't get a scream, you have the confirmation that the thing you

thought was contingent for your relationship never really was at all.

3. **I maintained healthy boundaries even with the important people in my life.** Some relationships go back so far that the idea that we'd hold that person accountable or, God forbid, consider ending the relationship seems super dramatic. Strangely, those years served sometimes lead us to give people grace proportionate to the amount of time they've been in our lives. Just because you played ball with Keith in fifth grade doesn't mean he gets a pass to take advantage of you or your family. Just because you're related to your aunt Sue doesn't mean she can get away with leeching off you. Know the lines you have to draw for everyone important in your life, the ones that keep your relationships about you and not what you can afford others, and then hold all your relationships (even those people you've known forever) to that standard.

CHAPTER 16

THE LIE:

I KNOW WHAT YOU'VE BEEN THROUGH

I grew up in a pretty homogenous town. By that, I mean every single person looked the same, believed the same, was the same. That's not a bad thing in and of itself, but it didn't serve me when I transitioned into the real world full of people of all different kinds. I'd never had any friends who were different from me when I was growing up. Really—all my friends were basically carbon copies of me and my family, which made anything else *different*. I see different now as exciting. But back then different was scary.

We fear the things we don't know.

I get now that there are bigger things at play than just my particular brand of personal ignorance. Structural and systemic inequities have existed for centuries and kept people in these homogeneous communities, out of community with each other, less available to understand what the other has gone through.

I just didn't get that back then.

When I got my first job out of college at 20th Century Fox, I sat in a cubicle next to a person who'd eventually become my best friend at work. We'd go to lunch most days, make inside jokes about how terrible certain things were in that work setting, the usual stuff. But it didn't start out that way. My cubicle neighbor happened to be gay, and I'd never talked to someone who was openly gay before, so I said and did things in the beginning of getting to know him that were a reflection of my ignorance and fear of the unknown. I asked questions that had to have seemed insensitive. I'm sure my inexperience with someone who did life unlike I did came right though. Frankly, I'm sure I came off like a know-it-all jerk at first, because that's how twenty-two-year-old me handled uncomfortable situations. In reality, it was me trying to find a comfortable rhythm with someone who represented something I didn't understand and didn't have any experience with.

Before I went on my first international trip for work, one of my older relatives, God rest her soul, asked me to come over to her house so she could give me some travel tips. I came in expecting to get the skinny on how to get the most out of a small budget, or how to use a Eurail pass, but instead I got this very serious warning: "Watch out for the Muslims." I mean, what? This relative had the best intentions in trying to keep me *safe*, but being Muslim or not has nothing to do with safety, and the fact that she'd never met a Muslim person in her entire life made her warning one based completely on fear and racism.

And that's the thing: we fear the things that are unfamiliar, that we don't know. They're foreign to us, and we think their foreign nature makes them something we should watch for since we don't know what to expect. There's no way around that, is there?

Of course there is.

If I'd grown up in a community that had exposed me to people who were gay, or if my relative had friends who were Muslim, that fear wouldn't have found expression. Because in that community with people who are "other" to us, we would have found connection and, in that connection, an empathy for their experience.

My wife and I adopted our youngest daughter in what was a happy ending to a harrowing five-year adoption journey. In the beginning we thought we'd adopt from Ethiopia. At the time, another couple from our church had successfully completed the international adoption process, and their success gave us confidence to step into the adoption space. There were so many things we didn't know, but the one thing we did feel fairly certain about was that if we were to successfully complete this mission, we would have a baby who did not look like us. We'd have a baby who had different skin color from ours, a different cultural background from ours, and different needs for connecting to who she was before she was part of our family. So we decided to find an intentional, multicultural community to learn all we could for our daughter-to-be.

I'm embarrassed to even write this out, but back then I thought I had a pretty good handle on race. I thought, because I'd read a book about Martin Luther King Jr. and watched a documentary on the civil rights movement and felt like a pretty aware person, that I had a decently solid grip on what it was to be a person of color in the twenty-first century. I wasn't overtly confident about it, but it was humbling to enter an environment that introduced me to a different life experience, to see how wrong I'd been. I thought I knew what it was like to be black in America but had never had the experience of truly doing life with someone who was black. How naive.

Our intentionally multicultural congregation invited people of all races to come together for worship and, as it turns out, real talk about daily life, current events, and the occasional push into harder conversations about racial reconciliation. This new community created friendships across the spectrum of race and had us learning every week from an African American pastor and sitting with people who shared the same interest in worship despite the variety of differences in each of our lives up to that point.

At first it didn't feel so different from other church experiences.

Then, in 2014, the names Eric Garner and Michael Brown and Tamir Rice became part of a different kind of conversation. A year earlier, stories on the news of kids getting shot would likely not have been something I spent as much time thinking about. They would have simply been news stories showing up on my feed. They probably would have struck me as sad, but I can honestly say I would not have given as much consideration to how these events affect people in their everyday, particularly people of color. But now, as I was trying to get a better handle on what to expect for our daughter of color, I witnessed firsthand how my friends in this community processed these headlines in ways I had not had to consider before.

I remember talking with a friend from church who asked me if I had ever considered having a conversation with my sons about what to do if they were pulled over. Like step-by-step, what to do to keep them safe. This dad was doing it in real time with his young children to prepare them for a world that greets them differently than it does me and mine, yet it had never occurred to me.

The world treats his kids differently. I thought I understood that on an intellectual level, but until I was talking with a friend, who had a name, in a seat next to me, it didn't land the way it should have. Black parents have a long history of teaching their kids how to interact with the police, and I never *really* knew that.

That reflects my reality to that point. That reflects my privilege. It provoked a different set of questions and a longer conversation about so many things. It led to a workshop on racial reconciliation. A church group took a civil rights tour through the South and brought back their stories. All of it stacked to confirm that not only did I not have any handle on race, but I will never, ever fully grasp it. All I could do was try to push into community to listen, learn, and connect with experiences I didn't have myself, to get closer to understanding.

I talked about this experience at Disney, and that led leadership to ask if I would consider being an executive sponsor of a black employee resource group. I wanted to learn about the experience of our employees of color, so I said yes and immersed myself in another environment that introduced me to things I hadn't previously thought about. We talked about a wide range of topics, from the kind of hair that would go on a doll from a Disney Channel show to ways to better connect with our customers of color. It was in this role as an executive sponsor that

I found myself in an extraordinary moment that will stick with me forever.

One afternoon a showrunner from ABC came on campus for a conversation about what they were cooking up for one of the shows in the next broadcast season. I made my way to my seat in the small theater and, about halfway through, I became aware of what I hadn't noticed, and frankly hadn't ever experienced, before. I was one of four white people in an auditorium of 220. I don't think I'd ever paid attention to the composition of an audience before that very moment—probably because I'd traditionally been in the majority. In a world where, more often than not, I'd been sitting with white men of a certain age, it had never occurred to me what it might feel like not to be like everyone else in the theater.

When we got to the question-and-answer portion of the program, I did not move. I had always been quick to throw my hand in the air in the past, but I didn't feel comfortable making an observation as someone who was different in the room. I stifled myself because of my difference and, for one of the first times, wondered if this was how someone who's a single person of color, one of the only women in the room, or a member of the LGBTQ community feels when they're outnumbered. That may not be the reality for everyone who identifies as a part of these or any groups, but the fact that it landed on me that way provoked a new set of questions I'd never considered before. It stuck with me. In a good way.

It led me to look actively for more ways to immerse myself in communities unlike mine to continue learning. When an opportunity presented itself to take a leadership position on a working women's initiative, I jumped. I wanted to hear about what it was like to be a woman trying to grow and thrive inside this great company I was working for. This came with some humbling introspection about the kind of team I'd built (not enough women as my direct reports) and affected the way I encouraged our female population to take prudent risks with projects and participate actively in meetings. It launched some work around an idea called "unconscious bias" where we tried to help our male employees be more conscious of some of the things they may inadvertently do to keep women from feeling they have as much opportunity, as much a voice, as open a seat at the table.

One of my prouder accomplishments at Disney was leaving my sales team, which had been historically male dominated, with more women than men on it. My successor was an amazing business leader who also happened to be a woman, who was the only female head of distribution in the industry at the time. It felt like the culmination of effort from all sides: her years of work and preparation to be the best candidate regardless of gender, my work in the women's taskforce informing how to build a better team, the company choosing a successor who backed up what they were preaching, all while setting records in an entirely new way.

Before I left Disney, they gave me an assignment that my first work colleague some twenty years back likely wouldn't have seen coming. It was a request to take on one final employee group. In my last year, I became Chief Ally for Disney's Pride group, the employee resource group for the LGBTQ community. In that capacity, as a straight ally of my gay colleagues, I got to hear how their life experiences affected them as employees of the company. As an executive I used my voice to represent their points of view as we considered how to drive the business forward. In the same way I had with my colleagues of color and women, I tried to model to other white male execs how building community with people who weren't like them might help them build a better team and solve problems with a more diverse set of perspectives and life experiences.

I don't tell you these stories to toot my own horn for leaning into communities that were different from mine. I tell you these stories because, if you ask me what has been one of the most satisfying things in my career, that helped me fulfill my purpose and even get ahead by staying out of my own way, it is connecting with people who are different from me. I've made a career on delivering solutions, and if you aren't in active community with someone different from you so you can learn what they need, you'll never be able to serve them well.

It didn't happen overnight, but this was a product of actively seeking out community, listening instead of talking, and humbling myself to never assume I knew the answers.

Rachel and I are building a company now based on the idea that we're better in community together. That through community, we can grow into fuller, more complete versions of ourselves. The first step to doing this is acknowledging that we don't know what you've been through. We don't understand what it is like walking in your shoes. We don't know how your life experience impacts your day-to-day, but we feel certain that the only way we'll get a little closer to understanding it is doing life together. Actively finding ways to spend time with those who don't think like us, or believe like us, so we can take the unfamiliarity and turn it into the empathy that comes from connection.

Don't want to lean into community with people who are

different from you because it's going to allow you to become a fuller, more complete human? Okay, then will you consider doing it because it will help you solve the problems in your business or life by bringing in new points of view?

One of my favorite podcasts is called *Reply All*. On one episode about hiring a diverse slate of humans for your team, they got into a conversation about ketchup.[1] It fundamentally changed the way I think about the importance of getting a bunch of different life experiences around me to help me navigate whatever this universe throws at me next.

Apparently, there are two types of people on this planet: those who put ketchup in the refrigerator and monsters who put it in the cupboard. If you had a team of people who exclusively did things like I do (cold ketchup) and found yourselves in an unfamiliar house and ran out of ketchup, every single person would look in the fridge—that's where ketchup is kept. It would not occur to anyone to check the cupboard, because none of them have any experience with that as the place where you store the red stuff. But, if there was someone who had a different life experience, someone who grew up in a house where the cupboard was the place, then the ketchup would be found and the crew would be able to eat fries in style.

It's a simple example of the beautiful thing that comes from community with different people. Different experiences act as a multiplier for possible solutions to problems.

So I'm working now to not only appreciate that others' experiences matter, but I'm debunking the lie that I know what you've been through. I'm working every day to learn a bit more of what it might mean to walk in your shoes, but I say that knowing that I've only ever walked in mine.

For me, that starts with acknowledging that I'm a man. I don't say that in the voice of Dwayne "The Rock" Johnson; I'm just clarifying that I wrote this from the perspective I've had in my life as a human born with a penis. That went sideways. "I'm not a woman," is another way of saying it. If you are a woman, I don't know what it means to have had your experience in life the way my wife might. I only know my own.

Secondly, I happen to be a Caucasian, heterosexual, able-bodied, Christian, American man. Said another way, I haven't had the journey that would allow me to know how a person of color, someone who's gay, someone who lives life with a physical disability, or someone who practices a different form of faith or grew up in a country with fewer freedoms than mine may have worked through what I have. I've never experienced grief from a loss in my immediate family. Never experienced the trauma some have while serving in our military. Don't know what it's like to battle depression. I have empathy and respect for those experiences, but I can't speak to what it's like to live any of those lives.

I don't claim to know it, but I do work to listen and understand.

You see, when those different life experiences introduce additional obstacles that might get in someone's way, particularly in ways I can't relate to or don't personally experience, that's a form of something in my life called *privilege*. I didn't fully appreciate this idea in my younger years, but it takes intentional work to understand why those obstacles exist for others . . . and how their lives are affected.

The younger, sheltered version of me didn't have the benefit of learning from a community with the vast array of experiences that exist in this world of ours. I needed a firsthand look at what it might be like to live life in a different way. It has been a game changer for how I approach just about everything. I'm grateful for that perspective shift. In fact, I was so grateful that I got a tattoo. It's a single word: ALLY. It sits on my right forearm just below my elbow and is a daily reminder to me, and more importantly my children. It means, *I'll stand with you and advocate for your worth*, especially if you don't have as loud a voice or enjoy the same access as I might have as a white, straight, male, able-bodied, Christian American.

I don't know what you've been through, but in the interest of showing up better in your life and the lives of people I care about, I'm going to try to understand a little bit more every day. I encourage you to consider how coming into community with people unlike you might help you become a better leader, friend, and contributor in this world of ours as well.

THINGS THAT HELPED ME

1. **I regularly surrounded myself with diverse community.** Every weekday Rachel and I do the strangest thing while hosting our morning show. *The Start Today Morning Show* is an online attempt to bring people of all kinds together with the common goal of reaching for more. We start most shows with the same words: "We are a community who comes together to reach for more and do so even though we don't look the same, act the same, vote the same, believe the same, or love the same. Sometimes we even grow because of those differences." If you put yourself deliberately in community with people who aren't like

you, it rounds off the rough edges of your fearful heart by showing you the humanity in people who are different from you.

2. **I invested time and money in communities of people unlike me.** In 2018 we established the Hollis Foundation as an attempt to divert 10 percent of company profits to organizations that support women, those in the military, children in foster care, and more. By leaning into these charitable organizations we're not only able to support causes close to our hearts, but we are also able to model for our children the importance of showing up for these communities in a way that allows us to connect to and develop empathy for them.

3. **I used my voice to demystify archaic thinking.** It is 2020, and people are still struggling with the idea that feminism is something all people should support. Despite the stigma it has in some circles, at its most basic, feminism is the suggestion that men and women are equal. Not that women are better than men or that women need to be strong or militant or anything. Just equal. I use my voice, platform, and model as a father to advocate for the equality of women. I do the same for any marginalized group, because I believe part of the responsibility of my privilege is trying to eliminate its existence altogether. And, if you bristle at the idea of this "privilege" talk, I'll challenge you to consider this quote that has been attributed to a couple dozen people: "When you're accustomed to privilege, equality feels like oppression." Let's not argue about it; just think about it.

CHAPTER 17

THE LIE:

THINGS THAT ARE POSSIBLE FOR OTHER PEOPLE AREN'T POSSIBLE FOR ME

Tall people can't be runners.

I wish I could tell you where I heard this notion, but it was something I was taught and believed. For thirty-six years of my life. It had something to do with hips or joints or how much weight you had to haul. At six foot, four inches tall, I was told running was a thing I couldn't or shouldn't do, so I didn't.

Then one day, out of nowhere, my right-hand at the office challenged me to a 5K race. We're both super competitive. He'd been a runner his whole life, but he was also few years older than I. I wasn't in great shape, but I liked the idea of showing him what youth and initiative could do.

He took me to school. Smoked me good. It was the perfect introduction to something I'd been told I couldn't do. It gave me motivation to see whether I could get better at it. That same colleague helped build the plan for my next race and the one after that. He helped me take a belief I'd clung to and throw it on its head.

Eight years later, I've run fourteen half marathons, including two on back-to-back weekends, and one "adventure marathon" in the wild hills of Ireland.

I am a runner. I am a tall runner.

I take to the roads every day.

The only thing that defines what you can become is you. Letting something external determine your worth or your trajectory is what is called a limiting belief. Limiting beliefs, in fact, are what all the chapters in this book are about: lies that hold us back in some way.

When I first heard this term it sounded like therapy-speak, like something someone who jumps up and down at a personal-development seminar at the local hotel ballroom talks through on the third Saturday of each month. But here's the thing: it's not that at all. It's not fancy. It's actually pretty simple. Limiting beliefs are things we mistakenly hold as truths about ourselves. As they inform our identities, they give us permission to pursue certain dreams, act in a certain way, have confidence or no confidence in our abilities, or think we do or don't have the right to do certain things. We think these are laws, that we have to learn to live within their bounds. But this is simply not the case.

You create the limits for what's possible in your life. You decide. You choose that reality. *You. Choose. That. Reality.*

We believe we have limitations for a whole host of reasons

we'll get to in a second, but when we believe these lies about what's possible, we rob ourselves. And, if we aren't aware of them, we'll never be able to fully get out of our own way. When we examine what it is we believe and why we believe it, the yield is transformational. It has been for me, and it will be for you as well.

So what are these limiting beliefs more specifically? They are the stories we believe that hold us back just by our giving them weight, those tracks that play on a loop in the background of our unconscious, telling us what we can or can't do. Examples include:

- believing this is just how things are (*They just don't hire people this old*);
- believing that, since you're not like someone else who does well in an area you'd like to do well in, it's just not possible for you (*I could never speak as well as he does, so I could never get that job*);
- identifying yourself as a person who has talent in one area that disqualifies you from the possibility of excelling in another area (*I'm in human resources, so I could never be good as a salesperson*);
- believing you can't do something even if you've never tried to do it (*I don't run, so I could never run a marathon*); and
- taking the principles from your childhood and the society you grew up in and automatically assuming they are true without testing (*Real men do or don't do . . . since that's how it was modeled by my dad, celebrated in society*, etc.).

The list could go on, but it's important to understand where you believe your worthiness comes from, what you believe you *can* or *can't do*, where you think your *permission to be you* comes from, and how your upbringing, societal norms, comparison to others, or foundations of identity create boundaries around what's possible. It's critical to see all this clearly. Once we do, then we must understand why we believe what we believe.

In my experience, most limitations are created from and rooted in fear. Fear of what other people will think. Fear of deviating from the norm. Fear of failure. Fear of rejection. Fear of being exposed as the work in progress that you are, of people finding out you're not that curated image of perfection you post daily on Instagram and Facebook. Insecurities about standing out in a way that could set you up for comparison, judgment, or ridicule are most of what keeps us marching to the beat of traditional norms. This is why humans tend to follow in the footsteps of the people we saw as mentors when we were young, or who we saw celebrated in media, the movies, or the press.

But we don't have to operate out of fear.

We've all had experiences that color how we think about what we can or can't be, how we should or shouldn't act. We've been in a bad relationship, and so there's a part of us that worries that other relationships will introduce the same pitfalls. We've had a work experience that wasn't great, so we assume other work environments come with the same traps. But this gives us the opportunity to find objective ways to see our life experiences and ask if the reservations we have are founded on something that actually applies to *all* similar situations going forward, or if we've only projected that they *could*. As we've talked about before, just because it happened once doesn't mean it will happen again—but if we're certain it will, that's the reality we'll live in. It will keep us from trying for a different outcome.

As my therapist likes to say, "The past doesn't predict the future," no matter how hard we try to control the possibilities of getting hurt, feeling shame, or carrying guilt.

My most recent battles with limiting beliefs came in times when I believed I was making well-thought-out decisions, but they turned out to be made against either a poorly constructed set of facts, a small sample size of data, or just bad reasoning.

As you learn to recognize the various limits you put on your life, it's going to take work to disentangle yourself from them. On a small scale, this might be because you've explained the benefits of your shortcut so confidently, you wouldn't dare admit you're totally lost even if you know you're driving in the wrong direction. On a bigger scale, it might be because you've taken a position for so long that you feel "pot committed" to it, that even if 4+4=9 isn't true, it doesn't matter because you've been saying it does for too long now to back down.

You can convince yourself of just about anything, and you'll make all kinds of arguments to keep from having to work harder or to shield yourself from encounters with discomfort that could make you grow.

Now, I'm not saying limits aren't real. Since the beginning of time, limits have existed. Limits keep people alive, and our brains are wired for survival. So limits are naturally going to exist in these brains of ours. The challenge, when we're talking about limiting beliefs, is to know which of the things we believe are really there for survival and which are manufactured beliefs that don't help us at all. If we don't do the work to ask the questions, we'll never know, and we'll just keep believing all of them absolutely to keep us safe, to keep us alive. But we can do better than that. Start now by identifying what it is you believe, which of those beliefs serve you, and which create unnecessary restraint that holds you captive, keeping you from where you want to go, keeping you from growth and ultimately fulfillment.

As the most decorated American Paralympic snowboarder Amy Purdy put it, "If we can see past preconceived limitations, then the possibilities are endless."[1] She has prosthetic legs. And wins Olympic medals. What's your excuse again?

Step 1: deliberately work to *know what you believe and why you believe it.*

Step 2: separate what you believe into things to keep believing and things to drop. *If it doesn't serve you and the ones you love, let it drop*, or move to step three and modify it.

Step 3: actively make changes to what you believe in the areas that hold you back. *Turn the limiting beliefs into empowering beliefs.* The way you position that hard thing you went through is everything.

The decision falls to you and you alone to believe in the truth that you are here for a reason, that you matter, and that the outside measures are nothing compared to your belief in yourself, the belief of your being enough. You have to know with outright certainty your importance in this world, regardless of what your job is, how you look, or what stories you're telling yourself. Don't let your limiting beliefs sell a version of your worthiness that underestimates what's possible for your life or chains you to a story that keeps you playing it safe, small, or not at all.

Know that you are enough today and every day, that you are capable and in control of what limits you'll adhere to, and use that knowledge to propel yourself forward in a way that maximizes your potential. You owe it not only to yourself but to those who matter to you most.

THINGS THAT HELPED ME

1. **I get back to the source of my truth on days I have a harder time believing it.** Are there days when I have insecurity about being enough? Of course. It's those days when I return to my faith, my wife, my kids, the feedback from my mentors, and the network who's been positively affected by my work. You have an array of similar relationships and sources of truth that remind you how worthy you are of your dreams and how capable you are of achieving them. Tap into those resources on the days when it gets harder to remember (trust me, those days will pop up) so you can maintain the momentum you'll need to build on that platform and achieve the impact you know you're capable of.

2. **I made an actual list of the lies I believed that kept getting in my way.** The table of contents of this book is a modified version of a list I started making on the way out of my first experience at that personal-development conference. To map where I wanted to go with my life, I had to start by identifying the specific things that might keep me from reaching my destination. It's an exercise that's worked so well that, at our RISE conference, my keynote is consistently on the topic of "What's going to get in your way." We encourage the audience to develop their plan for where

they want to take their lives, starting with what is likely to keep them from attaining their goals. It helps them build a plan considering what they'll need to navigate around. Make your list, and what you need to do to reframe the lies you believe to keep you out of your own way.

3. **I got a fresh perspective.** Have you ever been on a trip and had the epiphany that the things you thought were unchangeable or that gave you anxiety didn't exist in this parallel universe? On a few occasions, a trip for work landed me in another country and I realized that the people there have a totally different perspective on the things I might have determined I just needed to live with, and this realization affected me so much that it completely changed the way I thought about those things. If you aren't in the habit of disrupting your perspective for the benefit of seeing life through someone else's lens, put it on the calendar and force yourself outside your normal routine. Your mind will be blown.

CHAPTER 18

THE LIE:

I NEED TO PARENT LIKE MY PARENTS

There is a weird balance between what we think we do on our own and what we do because it's been programmed into us by forces outside ourselves. Those outside forces are particularly strong from our family of origin, be it functional or dysfunctional, present or absent, good or bad. When we do the work to understand why we do what we do, we also tend to realize we're allowed to have our own truth that best serves us and our families, separate from what we've accepted from our parents growing up.

Maybe that moment happened when you first moved away from your house and started asking bigger questions about who you wanted to be when you grew up. Maybe it was after a you were trying to unravel where things went wrong. Maybe that moment happened when you were first holding your own child, thinking about how you could guide them in today's world. Frankly, it was probably a combination of a host of moments that peeled back your consciousness like layers of an onion and allowed you to see the world differently.

Piggybacking on the last chapter, if for some reason you haven't had that "why you are the way you are" epiphany yet, do the work. Carve out some intentional time to uncover why you act and think the way you do. It wasn't until I really dived into my upbringing and my parents' values, their influence on my environment, and their impact on my worldview that I was able to ask better questions about what parts of my earlier life needed to be incorporated in my future. I recommend doing this diagnostic over and over as life introduces new seasons, new viewpoints, and new circumstances that may require you to adjust what you value and how those beliefs inform how you act.

In my journey, one of the biggest revelations was the notion that the way you think you have to be is influenced by other people. Modeled by other people. Ingrained in you without you even knowing it. These are unconscious thoughts that affect the things you say and the way you act. Everything from the way you show and receive love to the way you think about your self-worth. From your broader political ideology to where you fall on the optimist-pessimist spectrum. A fixed mindset versus a growth mindset. Extrinsic motivation versus intrinsic motivation. Limiting beliefs versus the truths that counter them.

All the things.

I happen to be the beneficiary of many more positive influences than negative. I have an awesome mom and dad who are both kind and supportive and have been there for me through-out my life. My mom was a stay-at-home mom of four kids who drove the carpool to youth group, and my dad was a hardwork-ing contractor who doubled as our baseball coach. My parents were the most significant shapers of what I believed growing up and because my early years were a positive experience, my instinct was to count myself lucky and to hold tightly to all the habits and values formed in those days. I thought of them as "good," having come from a quality source.

Somewhat counterintuitively, though, as I've grown and gotten more clarity on what works for me and my family, I have found not all of those early habits or values are necessarily what is best for my life today. At first, realizing that parts of how I was raised could be both good back then and also not how I want to raise my kids now took some work. The departure felt like a betrayal. The decision to make different choices to serve the needs of our family took time, but I had to make peace with the fact that "different" did not malign the past. It has been liberating and has afforded a family framework that makes sense for us.

For example, my parents are a reaction in many ways to their parents—my grandparents. All of them had a work ethic that reflected how they were raised in the aftermath of the Depression, through the uncertainty of world wars. Some of what my parents worry about is a result of what my grand-parents modeled, and that worry was, of course, both a good thing and a bad thing. I can see clearly that my practicality, the worrier I've been in my life, as well as some of my bent toward a fixed mindset, all come from things that were passed down generation to generation. Some of those things have served me, and some have held me back. All have made me who I am.

But I don't have to feel chained to them.

In the same way you need to work through which of your limiting beliefs you need to drop or flip to empowering, you also need to do the same with values and habits from your family of origin.

Which pieces of your parents' style serve you and your family both now and into the future? That goes for the things you've assigned as good stuff as much as bad stuff. Decide to do what makes sense for your life, your family, this year, in your town, with your set of circumstances—those decisions are yours to make. And, as it turns out, making a departure from your past, even a positive one, doesn't mean you don't have respect and appreciation for the things that made you who you are. It simply means you need additional or different things to thrive in a world that's different now from the one you grew up in.

Your parents will likely feel uneasy with your departure from the way they parented at some point. Most do, and that's okay. They aren't raising your kids. You are.

Your parents may express concern about your career choices, and that's okay too. Their worry is most likely a sign of love, but they won't have to live with the regret of not chasing your dreams. You will.

Frankly, you may find that you don't agree on how you vote, how you experience your faith from one denomination to the next, how you think about gender roles in 2020, the impact of carbon on global warming, or on Star Trek versus Star Wars. Whatever your version of different is, get comfortable with it all being okay. Just be smart about how (or if) you bring up any of it at Thanksgiving if you want to be invited back.

Little Dave who was raised in his parents' home is wildly

different from Dave of today. Those differences are things I'm proud of now, and they in no way marginalize the impact of what it was like to be supported as I was growing up.

I wasn't always this confident. In fact, I struggled with self-confidence for a long time. I lived in fear of hurting the feelings of the people who had devoted time to instilling what they did in me. I worried that in some way they might read my independence and decision to pursue something different for my life as a backhanded insult of how they lived. That first decade transitioning from living in my parents' house to living in mine was clunky, but it wouldn't have been if I had known then what I know now:

Times are different. People are different. Needs are different.

Give yourself permission to take only the things from your family of origin that propel you into being who you were put on this earth to be. Make peace with those differences. This is true for those of you who grew up like me and also true for those of you who didn't have the luxury of parents who were together, who loved each other, who were supportive. You may have come out of brokenness, and the decision to parent in a way that serves your family is one you're going to have to actively make every day—to take the good that came out of your harder circumstances and refuse to see the bad as a sentence you're destined to repeat.

So make peace with the idea of making different choices. Then prepare yourself and your kids for their eventual departure from the way you raised them as they seek the same mix of what's right for their family—some of what you bestowed on them and some that they jettison as they make their own way.

Don't be afraid to move toward something different from

what you've known. Your kids need to be parented by you in the way you know they need best. It will be wholly unique to every other set of parents, including your own, and as a result will make your kids uniquely prepared to take on this world.

THINGS THAT HELPED ME

1. **I kept the most important thing the most important thing.** If you live your life to make sure that others approve, that even your parents approve, it might come at the expense of the most important thing: giving your kids the tools they need to grow into who you hope they'll become. The benefit of time has changed the things I thought I knew. Those changes didn't just happen when I went from living at my parents' house to being out on my own; they're continually evolving as I push through this journey of life. The things I thought even just two years ago are wildly different from what they are today— thank goodness for that. As you stay focused on the most important things, you'll likely continue to redefine what you and your family need and how those needs change as life continues in new and different ways.

2. **I changed my environment to get clearer context.** Leaving my industry, moving my family, taking on a new line of work with my partner—all these things challenged the way I used to think. All these things gave me context for what matters now and, maybe more importantly, what no longer matters at all. The list of things I once valued that no longer serve me or my family is too long a list to fit

in this book, but it wasn't until I changed my environment that I was actually able to see those things for what they were. Find a way to get some context, and see if you don't think differently about things.

3. **I reminded myself of my critics' intentions.** When my parents were disappointed in decisions I made in my life, their disappointment came because they wanted me to avoid pain, and they worried about the influence I might have as an older brother to three younger siblings. When feedback comes from a place of love, take it at face value and decide if it applies to your life objectively. When someone on the internet invokes their beliefs to tell me that I'm not living my life the way I should, rather than get defensive I try to remind myself that their intention is to help me, even if it wasn't received that way. Sure, there are trolls who have nothing but malice intended, but I'd prefer to believe in a world where people are advocating more for what they believe is good than anything else. If they're really coming from that place, even if we disagree, it's easier to accept the friction when I consider their intentions.

CHAPTER 19

THE LIE:

I CAN ACHIEVE BALANCE IF I WORK HARD ENOUGH

Bigfoot. Loch Ness monster. Balance. What do all three of these have in common? They're all rumored to exist, have forever been tracked, have seemingly been captured for fleeting moments, and, alas, are fables. None of them exist, and the sooner you accept that balance is among the things you cannot actually attain or control in your life, the sooner you'll find yourself in a more productive, peaceful, and reasonable state of mind. Be free.

When I'm on a panel, I always get questions about balance.

"So, four kids, successful marriage, successful business, how do you do it all?"

I always go back to a two-part answer.

The first thing is acknowledging that I do not do it all. My wife and I do not do it all. Nobody does, and someone on Instagram telling you otherwise is ridiculous.

Anyone who has ambition for this many spinning plates does it with a community of people, family, and friends as a support system. As taboo as it may be to talk about this in some circles, the only way Rachel and I can pursue the ambitious calling on our lives is with the help of a nanny and the occasional babysitter. We both have roles with the company and our various partners that sometimes pull us out of town, so we have help—and we are okay talking about it. We're okay dealing with people, including our own families, who might judge the way we've decided to live our lives relative to how they might, because we do what's right for our family and this mission, not theirs. Chasing the great passions of our life, delivering value to a broad audience, using our potential for impact? Those opportunities come with trade-offs. When you find yourself chasing this kind of work, you will need help.

The second and maybe more important part of the answer is that we've become comfortable with the reality that balance is not possible. Balance is something you strive for on the whole but, on any individual day, it doesn't really show up. Some days our work is going to pull us further from the kind of quality time we wish for every day with each other. Other days work doesn't do that, and it allows us to fully engage and be a part of every single one of all four kids' needs and wants. Some days work gets sacrificed, because being in the front row of a fourth-grade production of *Moana* at 11:20 a.m. matters. It's not necessarily normal to have consecutive weeks where life is the same way every day.

Because of this, achieving perfect balance is not a possibility. Instead, the goal is to *stay centered* to handle the variability of what life throws our way. So what do we do to help us juggle everything in a healthy way?

FRONT-LOADING

The only way we can survive the pace and occasional chaos of our business and the ever-changing needs of our household is by being extraordinarily intentional in how we plan. We have to acknowledge in meticulous detail what's coming in the days and weeks ahead. We prepare each other and each of our kids, as well as the members of our team, for what to expect before it happens. We call that front-loading.

For us, it's a process that starts over every Sunday night when my wife and I sit down with our calendars and go day by day, hour by hour, and plan out what each of the kids has with school and sports, our meetings and travel, household responsibilities, and what personal goals we want to hit. Down to the minute. We look at our individual calendars and have a conversation about who is available to drive the kids to school on this day, or take one of the kids to practice on that day. We do this checking in because we are each as responsible as the other for raising our humans. My responsibility is 100 percent. My wife's responsibility is 100 percent. We are equally responsible for raising these children, but doing it requires us to acknowledge that we're not both going to be available to do it on an every-day or every-week basis.

To institute this practice, we have to find a time to have

those conversations. We don't wait until bedtime to determine who is going to be putting the kids to bed, or until it's time to drive the kids to school to determine who's going to take them. This is important, because if you wait to say, "Hey, do you mind taking Noah to the doctor today?" the person receiving that request last minute might hear it as, *I value my time and my priorities on my calendar more than I value yours. I'm going to delegate the responsibility of caring for our kid to you because of that value assessment I've just made.* This may not have been the intention, but it just might be the way it's received. Planning the week's schedule on a Sunday, when it's not the day of, allows us to take some of the emotion out of that conversation.

Front-loading. Creating equilibrium in an imbalanced, chaotic world. Remember, the only time anyone gets upset is when they're surprised by something. It's especially true when you're trying to have an exceptional relationship with your partner.

SELF-CARE

Even though the first step in staying centered is managing expectations, self-care is just as, or more, important.

As a recovering codependent dad and husband, I used to connect my wife's or kids' happiness to my happiness. That meant I felt guilty for taking time away for myself, usually so much that I sacrificed it for what I thought catered to what they needed. As a result, I didn't work out as often, didn't take as many mental-health breaks, didn't invest in time with friends, and the net was a weaker version of me. A dad with no energy. A husband with no pep. It wasn't until we came to see how important health is as a foundation for unlocking everything else we want to do for each other that we forced it front and center and made it a focal point, ensuring our calendar was a reflection of how we might refuel for everyone who was counting on us.

Same Sunday routine: When are you, Dave, going to the gym? When are you, Rachel, going on a run? What are we eating every single night? To start every week, we meal plan for every single day and talk about what days and what times we are working out. It creates accountability, but it also makes sure we stick to our belief that if we aren't showing up for ourselves and pouring into our health, I cannot be the husband Rachel deserves or the father my kids need, and the same for Rachel as a wife and mother.

Rachel and I talk often of the mid-twentieth-century military adage "Hope is not a strategy." You have to plan how you're going to be healthy, how you're going to care for yourself. You can't simply hope that you're going to make healthy choices in the midst of a chaotic day with four kids. It will not just happen. Don't hope that you're going to find time to refuel; plan for when that time is going to be.

RELATIONSHIP INVESTMENT

Once you set your intentions with front-loading and have properly focused on self-care, how else can you remain centered in the middle of, well, life? By actively pursuing your most critical relationships. This means intentionally investing in your partner, spending quality time with your kids, and building deeper connections with a few meaningful friends.

When our oldest was maybe a year old, Rachel and I realized that if we didn't have a regular date night, we were going to be inconsistent in how we connected. Intimacy isn't just what happens in the bedroom. Intimacy is what happens when you pause living life for others and pursue life for you as a couple. Rachel and I do date night every single Thursday night. This means we have arranged sitters for Thursday nights between now and the end of time and have conditioned our kids to expect us to go out then. Are there times when our kids are like, "Man, you're going on a date?" Of course. Frankly, it's not even a conversation any longer, because the answer is always, "You're darn right, we're going on a date, because we love each other and the only way we can be the best parents for you is if we are as strong as we can be as a couple."

Rachel and I are modeling for these four human beings the way we hope they show up as adults. This includes the practice of dating your spouse, the practice of intentionally putting yourself in an environment that says "Put on your fancy underwear" on a regular basis, the practice of going out and doing things that are an adventure of some kind and maybe disrupt your routine. Those are things we want our kids to do and model for their kids when they are in relationships.

We also take two trips a year. We take one trip with our whole family, and then we take a vacation without the kids. As I wrote this, our kids knew we had our December family trip planned, as well as an adults-only getaway scheduled for just after the New Year. Family trips are not necessarily relaxing trips for the parents who are manning four kids on the road with suitcases, and diapers, and everything else. It doesn't mean we don't have fun. Of course we have a great time, play games, give the kids one-on-one attention, and do all the fun things. But when it comes to the other trip, it's not a trip. It's a vacation. It's where Rachel and I say goodbye to the small human beings. We're going to refuel so we can come back and be the kind of parents they all deserve, because we love each other.

When we take the time to intentionally invest in our relationships, we can find that elusive sense of peace in the middle of life's craziness. Even if true balance is not something we can ever attain in this life, we can still find a more productive, reasonable state of mind by prioritizing and putting some simple habits into practice.

THINGS THAT HELPED ME

1. **I got over guilt.** Guilt, a lot of times, is informed by the opinion of someone you've given power to. Your guilt isn't even necessarily a thing that you feel. It's a thing you were taught to feel. So if you feel guilty about leaving your kids at home to go to work, it might be because of the passive-aggressive comments your mother-in-law makes. You're deciding to let her tell you how to raise them. In our family, it starts with this idea that if you're not in this house raising these kids with us, respectfully, you don't get a say in how we do it. *Thank you for offering your opinion, but we're going to do what we think is best for our kids.* So whenever I start feeling guilty about something, I go to that first question: Where is the guilt coming from, and should I be giving that source power over me?

2. **I created milestones to look forward to.** Because life

is chaotic, my family had to have things to look forward to so, in the times when it felt overwhelming or hard, we could couch those feelings against a time in the future when we'd be pausing life to refuel our batteries. These didn't need to be big things, but by making sure our calendar was a reflection of the kind of marriage Rachel and I wanted to have, or the kind of quality family moments we knew could create memories, we always had things to keep us going.

3. **I committed to nonnegotiables.** To find a healthier way to juggle the chaos of time, I had to put down some hard rules and boundaries to live by. We eat dinner as a family at the dinner table every night at 6:30 pm. If there's a meeting that evening, that meeting has to end in time to get us around the table. I also committed to moving my body every single day. Every. Single. Day. The only way I'll be able to have the stamina to show up well for the people in my imbalanced life is if I start with a foundation of feeling well myself. The list goes on, but the point is to set the nonnegotiables and then commit to them doggedly.

THE LIE:

MENTAL HEALTH ISN'T AS IMPORTANT AS PHYSICAL HEALTH

October 10 is World Mental Health Day. Each year there's a theme—recent themes have included suicide prevention (2019), young people and mental health in a changing world (2018), and mental health in the workplace (2017). The day is sponsored by the World Health Organization and exists to educate people and generally support mental health.

It's not a widely celebrated day.

In a world where it seems like we're celebrating something every day (National Angel Food Cake Day also falls on October 10), it's easy to gloss over any of these days without taking time to think about why they exist. But the fact that this day is set aside in the first place is the reason why this chapter and its lie are so important. I believe part of the reason why we have a World Mental Health Day is to remind people that mental health is something that needs to be talked about, and I want us to get to a place where we are more comfortable having that conversation. We shouldn't have to convince people that mental health is as important as physical health.

For example, if you had a pain in your side for three days, you would go to the doctor and have it looked at. But some of you have been carrying around a pain in your heart or your brain for decades, yet you refuse to go see someone who could actually address the problem. Please know that there are tools and doctors available to you. If there are resources that exist, and you refuse to use them but then wonder why you're still struggling—that is a choice you have made not to address the problem.

Mental health and mental illness affect everyone, whether it is you personally or someone you love. And yet, because of the taboos around the topic, getting the necessary help is still a struggle for those who need it most. It's part of the reason why the second leading cause of death among young people is suicide. Consider that the National Institute of Mental Health estimates nearly one in five lives with a mental illness.[1] The National Council of Behavioral Health suggests that almost half of adults (46.4 percent) will experience a mental illness during their lifetime but only 41 percent of people who've had a mental disorder in the past year received professional health care or other services.[2] If we want to change those kinds of statistics, we have to take control of the narrative and normalize the conversation around mental health.

If you are reading this, you are human and that means you have to work on your mental health. That in no way means you are broken or that there's something wrong with you. It's just a fact. All of us—every single person, including me—struggle. And the reason why I can get past the struggle is that I have become comfortable raising my hand and saying, "Hey, I am struggling. I need help." And I no longer have a stigma around mental health, because mental health and physical health are now just *health* to me.

There seems to be this wild assumption that working on your mental health indicates that you aren't an awesome human being, or you are less than. I don't believe this. Think about it this way: if you were working on your physical health so you could run a marathon or climb a mountain, you would probably tell every human on the planet because you would be so proud of pushing yourself physically to be healthy. So why not think about mental health the same way? Get out of your own way, let go of the stigma, and believe that you are awesome *because* you are pursuing health in all the ways—mentally and physically. I now brag about going to a therapist as much as I would brag about climbing a mountain or training for a marathon, because that therapy—that work that I've done on the mental side of the ledger—is as important in unlocking the great parts of my life as anything else.

If you stay stuck inside the lie that tells you that admitting you struggle makes you weak, you will never get help. When I first went to therapy, I didn't think I wanted to go, and I was ashamed of needing help and what other people might think about it. But once I realized how much good came from it, I told everyone. And if someone gave me a look like, "Oh, really? You go to therapy?" I would say, "You're dang right I go to therapy, and you should go to therapy, too, because therapy is the thing that is currently helping me climb out of a valley that I'm stuck in."

Bottom line: If you want to be a healthy human, you need to pursue mental health just as you would physical health. See a professional if necessary. Therapy is one of the greatest gifts I've ever given myself. Period. Go. Please go. It will literally change your life.

———

So how do you tend to your mental health? You can start with the free resources that exist on mentalhealth.gov or by searching for mental health hashtags on social media. There are so many fantastic resources that exist for free.

In addition to finding the right tools, I think the mental health journey starts by going back to the basics: get enough rest; make sure you are eating regularly; see a doctor if you need one; take medicine if it's needed; confide in someone you can trust; and find the space to process what you're feeling. Basics.

In our online community, we talk often about our "5 to Thrive." These five daily actions put us in a position to get the most out of each day. Each of these things is as much about mental health as anything else:

- **Practice daily gratitude:** wire your brain to be on the hunt for good.

- **Wake up an hour early to focus on you:** practice prayer and meditation and focus on goals before your day—and the chaos—starts in earnest.
- **Move your body for thirty minutes:** push yourself physically to change the way you feel mentally and emotionally.
- **Give up a category of food you know you shouldn't eat:** realize the power of making and keeping a promise to yourself.
- **Drink half your body weight in ounces of water:** the brain is 75 percent water, and dehydration slows circulation that can affect how we think and feel.

Beyond our 5 to Thrive, what else can you do?

- **Make yourself a priority.** You may bristle at this, but it needs to be said: you need to be your first priority. You cannot pour out of an empty cup. So many of you feel like you don't have the time, feel overwhelmed, or feel as though you're drowning inside of anxiety, because you are saying "yes" to others' priorities at the expense of yours. You need to put on your oxygen mask first. This doesn't make you selfish; this makes you responsible. Show up for you first, and you'll be able to show up for the rest of your life well.
- **Perform a regular self-audit.** Check in with yourself frequently. You need to know how you are doing. In your calendar right now, put a regular reminder that says self-audit, and make it a recurring meeting every three months. Then sit down and be really honest with yourself. Once

you get to the bottom of how you're doing, *take action*. If you are struggling in an area, you need to raise your hand and ask for help. You know who doesn't get help? The person who doesn't ask for it.

- **Acknowledge the truth of your experience.** There's something about this curated world we all live in that has us wanting to convince people that things aren't so bad— "Trust me, it's all good." But sometimes what someone really needs to hear is, "It was terrible, but I'm strong for having gone through it. It was impossible and I'm still grieving, but I am a little better every day." Don't believe the lie that if you just bury it deep enough, it'll go away. Not addressing the things we're holding onto allows them to stew and turn toxic in a way that ends up rotting the inside. It's okay to acknowledge the truth of a terrible experience. It's okay to admit that it's freaking hard. The sooner you can become comfortable with admitting it, the sooner you might actually be able to process it and move a bit further away from feeling like there's a weight you'll never get out from under. Get past the ego, the pride, and the fear of someone else's judgment and take a step closer to owning who you are. Have confidence that there may, in fact, be someone who needs to hear your stories so that they can also have the courage to pull themselves out of the place they're in.

- **Embrace the reality that struggle is universal.** Quit believing the lie that there are certain people who struggle and certain people who don't. Everyone has issues. If you're breathing on this planet and pursuing great things, you're going to struggle on an almost-daily basis, and that does not make you broken.

- **Get creative.** Literally do something creative as an outlet. Find a way to express yourself. Writing this book was a form of therapy. I expressed my creativity and processed my experience in the most cathartic way possible—by telling everyone the lies I was believing that kept me trapped in shame and insecurity. Now that it's all out there, it liberates me to pursue being the best possible version of myself. I've used this outlet to tell every story, and if someone wants to judge me for being honest about how I got through my struggle, they aren't going to be part of my life. I do not care. I'm free.

- **Have and keep boundaries.** You have to make sure you have fortified boundaries around your calendar, your social feed, your personal space, and your mind. Mental health is as much about restricting the things that come into your life as it is about anything else. If you don't currently have a set of boundaries that affords you the space you need, or you find it difficult to say no when someone is trying to infiltrate the sanctity of your space, then you need to reinforce your boundaries. Get really comfortable saying no to people who ask you to do things that are contradictory to your value set.

- **Own your weakness and get help.** When I was struggling the most, the only way I was able to get out of my own way, the only way I was able to get help, was by raising my hand and having a conversation in total honesty. That was scary and hard, but you can't expect people to be able to read your mind. Managing the way they think about you doesn't serve you. If you are hurting, become comfortable with being a little more transparent and honest, especially with people who are in your circle and you trust the most.

- **Ask someone how they're doing.** Every single day, ask somebody how they're doing, and when they say fine, then you ask them, "How are you really doing?" Every single day, if you go to an office, there are people who are hanging on by a thread. You don't know what a difference it might make in someone's life if you actively listen to how they are doing. Offering to help someone else will change the way you think about asking for help when you start seeing the impact it has on others.

- **Give yourself permission to take medication if you need to.** This is one of those things people will inevitably want to argue about, but there are countless examples of people who have taken antianxiety meds or antidepressants to get through a rough season and found them to be lifesaving help when they needed it most. If you are struggling and have a stigma around taking medication for a mental health struggle, you need to know that it's okay to get the help you need.

- **Get into a community that will listen to and support you.** Community has changed the way I carry around the weight of whatever it is I'm feeling when I'm not okay. I get to okay faster by acknowledging that I don't have it together all the time. It's okay to share your hurts; it's okay to talk openly about the things you are struggling with. The Hollis Company has created an online community full of people who are supportive if you need to share your experience with others. We host Rachel's private Facebook group called Made for More where hundreds of thousands of people from all different life experiences come together to share and support. There are people who will love on you. They will tell you, as you admit your struggle, that sharing your struggle doesn't make you weak or broken. It makes you a very normal person that they have empathy for because they can relate. If not our community, plug into one at work, school, church, or online, and stay connected in way that helps you see how normal it is for you to work through the difficult stuff in your life.

- **Give yourself permission to get through hard days in your own way.** It's okay to have bad days. When they come, it's okay to do what's best for you. It's okay to do the thing you need to do in the season you are in. As much as other people are going to give you tips, as much as there may be a conventional way things are done, you have to become comfortable doing what is best for you and what is best for your family.

Mental health is just health. It's as important as physical health and should be treated as such. Once we push past the taboos that exist around mental health, a healthy life can then be about doing the work, finding the community, changing our mindset, and asking for help when we need it. If you're struggling, please know you are not alone. Your struggle is a sign of your humanity. Your willingness to raise your hand and acknowledge that you're struggling is a sign of your strength.

I hope you can find that strength.

STAY OUT OF YOUR OWN WAY WITH INTENTION AND DISCIPLINE

Twenty lies later, and what have we learned? We can often be our own worst enemies. When we find ourselves stuck or unfulfilled or just getting through life, it's easy to think that's just the way things are. It lets us off the hook if we can blame it on how we're wired, or that we didn't have the kind of luck that someone else may have had. If we can assign responsibility to forces we decide are out of our control, we don't have to take responsibility for doing anything about being stuck. We spin our wheels in a mediocre station in life not because it's our destiny but because we've made it so. When we think we'll finally get beyond the "just okay" version of ourselves only when *this* happens or *that* happens, we give all our power to outside forces and surrender the possibilities of an exceptional life to the chance that it might happen.

Lean in close: it won't. An exceptional life doesn't just happen. An exceptional life is something that takes work. Intentional work. Disciplined work. Work that you'll have to do every single day in the pursuit of being better tomorrow than you are today. Better tomorrow: that's the goal and the secret to true fulfillment. When you wake up knowing you've made progress from where you were yesterday, that's when you'll feel a sense of accomplishment. The momentum of your efforts is the definition of growth, and ultimately that growth is the foundation for your fulfillment.

Every one of these lies we've been working through together was based on a universal truth: *I* was at the root of what kept tripping me up. Now I know that there are roadblocks in society that make it much more difficult for some than it was for me, but what I am talking about are the things I could control, the lies I believed, internal roadblocks I had to deal with no matter my background.

I'm grateful that I now have the perspective to see not only that it was me that kept getting in my own way, but that I could have avoided falling down with a bit more intention and discipline. And I can start to avoid it now. So let's end this book by identifying five areas that, if you were to get a handle on them, would help you avoid the dumb stuff we tend to do and instead pursue a greater life:

- Define Your **Operating Principles**
- Commit to **Habits** That Fuel You
- Find the **Leverage** to Live No Other Way
- Be Deliberate in What You **Focus** On
- Surround Yourself with **Relationships That Serve You**

These basic building blocks may sound a little simple, and that's the point. As a personal-development newbie, I needed things that were simple, that anyone could do. That said, it's important you hear these words: simple doesn't mean ineffective. Simple doesn't equate to limited impact when applied to your life. If you were to fully embrace two of these five things, you would have a better life. Let's dig in.

DEFINE YOUR OPERATING PRINCIPLES

When I worked at the Walt Disney Company, I had twelve different jobs over seventeen years. That meant eleven times, a group of people was pulled into a conference room with some degree of anxiety as they waited on the news of who their new leader was going to be. After the second or third time, I realized it was taking nearly the entirety of my engagement with a team to get them to a place where they understood who I was, how I led, what I expected of them in how they did their jobs, and the kind of culture I was hoping to have in that department or division. I needed a way to fast-track the getting-to-know-you portion of my time with new teams, so I decided that if I could create a cheat sheet to accelerate that process, it would be a win on all sides.

So I did just that. I made a list of what I called *operating principles*, and the next time I found myself in a first meeting with a new team, I walked through them. These principles are a reflection of the truths in my life.

Truths. You see, I decided to start with this one of the five building blocks because of the chapters we've just come out of.

The antidote to the lies that we tell ourselves? The truths that make those lies impossible to believe. As I look at this list of operating principles now, I can see that each principle was born out of a time when I created imbalance, stumbled, made things take longer, or created friction in my relationships by not living to that standard. Trial and error over twenty-five years in the entertainment business created a roadmap, my list of truths that can apply to all areas of life:

1. **Work to live; don't live to work.** If you do something you're passionate about without making time for your family and yourself, you'll never be successful.
2. **Find a mentor you trust.** You need someone who will champion your growth in the organization and in life.
3. **Take assignments that put you out of your comfort zone.** Growth happens outside your comfort zone, and you cannot be fulfilled if you aren't growing.
4. **Do more than one thing with your career.** Whether you work in PR, research, marketing, sales, or anything else, a renaissance man or woman is more valuable, marketable, and relied upon in any organization.
5. **Develop initiatives, name them, represent their value, and update the organization as you progress.** Be a humble champion of and create visible momentum for the value you deliver to the team.
6. **Surround yourself with strong people, and let them shine.** It makes you look better when you give credit. On the flipside, focus on how your efforts can accelerate your boss's promotion and not your own—you'll find yourself promoted faster when you do.

7. **Deliver honest feedback regularly (both up and down), deploying radical candor in a considerate way.** Be genuine and empathetic in how you deliver feedback and how you hope to be received.

8. **Act with integrity, then don't worry about what anyone else thinks of you.** But do 360s and ask for feedback from people with mastery in areas where you want to grow and understand how to be better.

9. **Be a solution provider.** Understand the objectives of the customer (internal or external), and meet needs to that end.

10. **Commit to truth.** Demand your teams represent problems in an environment that does not penalize them for having them, but do insist that they come with solutions. The only time anyone ever gets upset is when they're surprised by an outcome—manage expectations honestly.

You'll have to decide which of these apply well to your station in life. Can't find a mentor? Start with books, podcasts, social media, and YouTube videos from voices that push you to think differently and grow. You don't take assignments from someone else? Take the initiative to push yourself into a challenge. You don't think you have a "traditional" career to do more than one thing with? This applies to you, too, stay-at-home mom or dad. Your roles will continue to adapt through the life stages of your kids. The more you're intentionally adding to your set of parenting skills, the better you'll be able to equip them well.

This practice with teams in a work environment has transitioned into a personal goal-setting practice in my personal life as well. In the Hollis Company's *Start Today Journal*, we do a

daily, repeated prompt about how the ten-years-from-now version of ourselves would show up today to make goals happen.

In the journal, we ask for these single-line statements that
can be about big audacious goals. Then we ask:

*If these statements are true, how do I need to behave today
to make them so?*

My entry this morning includes, "The Hollis Company
employs one thousand people," and "Our charitable foundation gives away $10 million a year," but also has simple personal
proclamations like, "I'm an exceptional husband who actively
pursues his wife," "I'm a present, involved dad who makes eye
contact and has conversation without technology," and "I am in
sick physical shape from working out every single day." These
declarations set my intention each morning for how I would like
to operate for the day.

List the goals that, if followed, set you and those around
you up for success. I share my personal entries each day with
my wife and, even in this bizarre world we live in, on social
media, because it creates accountability. Yes, I'm trying to wire
my brain to believe that I am goal-oriented and accountable,
even on the days I don't want to, especially on the days it's hard
to be that way. Each of these things is written in the present
tense as a hack for our subconscious to look for ways to make
them real from one minute to the next.

In the same way the kickoff meetings with my teams set the
bar for what was expected, they also clearly drew boundaries
around what wasn't expected. If you do the things on the list,
you don't do the opposite of those things. And if you incorporate
this into your life, when you find yourself veering into areas that
contradict what you've told yourself, your team, your spouse,

or any supporter you are, you will be able to snap yourself back more quickly into that version of you that you know you need to be.

The big question for you: Do you know your operating principles? If you aren't clear on what you believe, on your truths, the chances of your avoiding the lies that trip you up are unbelievably higher. Motivation guru Zig Ziglar famously said, "If you aim at nothing, you'll hit it every time."[1] It's true. So, *make your list*. How would the version of who you hope to be show up for your family today? What version of you gets the greatest yield out of your team as their boss, out of your small humans as their parent? When you look yourself in the mirror, who do you hope to see, and how are the guardrails you're putting around your life helping deliver that more exceptional, more fulfilled version of you?

COMMIT TO HABITS THAT FUEL YOU

Now hear this: you are not running your life; *your habits are*. On the back end of Pixar's *Inside Out* trying to explain how the brain works, a 2015 *Time* article reminds us what scientists have been saying for years: "Never mind the five characters controlling your thoughts, *you* barely control them. It's the unconscious that's really in charge."[2] Without thinking about it, you're going through your day making decisions and acting on the stimulus that drops in front of you; you might believe you're in control, but really it's just the muscle memory of your mind, searching for how you've previously handled a scenario that looked like this one and replicating it over and over again.

If you haven't done any work to understand what habits are and why they're an important thing to get a handle on, do yourself a life-changing favor and start there. Read *The Power of Habit* by Charles Duhigg as the first step.[3] In the book, he breaks down how, in life, we are all triggered by events. At some point in our day we have a cue that sets off an action. That reaction is our routine, which produces a feeling of satisfaction—a reward, if you will. That's the loop: cue, routine, reward. Cue, routine, reward. Sometimes a good routine, sometimes a bad routine. Primarily unconscious. You're likely not even aware of it unless you really stop to think about it.

In the pursuit of turning bad unconscious habits into good conscious habits, identifying the trigger is the first step. What is it that sets your action into motion? Duhigg did experiments that showed there were basically five prompts that consistently provoke your routine, and they've been helpful in my experience as I try to understand where my triggers exist, at least the cues that trigger a bad habit. They are *location, time, other people, emotional state*, and *immediately preceding action*. When I first read this book, I turned these prompts into an exercise to list the times I wished I'd made better decisions and attempted to connect the dots to find consistent patterns.

- **Location:** Are there places that elicit a mindset change? For me, when we had two kids under two, pulling into the driveway was a cue for feeling like I needed a drink to brave a night of less sleep, crying humans, and a mama who was going to have the same feelings of exasperation.
- **Time:** For twenty-five years I worked in offices where

there were snacks in every common area, in a file cabinet near my desk, and left out by a conference room. For twenty-five years, 3:00 p.m. was a time just long enough after lunch that had me wandering the halls looking for trouble. I could be on the best eating program and yet, like a zombie, at the strike of three, I'd find myself carb-loading in a conference room.

- **Emotional state:** When I'm feeling insecure, I turn to humor. Good news, I'm really funny. Bad news, deploying my humor when I feel threatened in a scenario is a thinly veiled attempt at using one of my strengths to overcome something I perceive as a weakness, at the expense of others.
- **Other people:** We all have certain people who can set us off even if we just think of them. I've had bosses who were a trigger, extended family, toxic friends, and even, as described above, my small humans.
- **Immediately preceding action:** Feedback is a thing I need and a thing I tend to process better now, but I still struggle with it. It could be from my wife, an employee, or a customer from the internet buying something from the Hollis Company. As much as I need that feedback to adapt and grow, my initial reaction to hearing feedback can set me off.

The question here is, where are you at your best and where are you at your worst? What is it about that place, time, or other element that provokes that response, and what is it about that response that provides a reward? Is there an alternative response that could still leave you feeling the reward? Is there a way to plan how you're going to show up in an area before you're in front of that cue? Of course, that's the goal.

Start by identifying your triggers.

Ask if the response to those cues serves you or not.

If the response doesn't serve you, how do you create a new routine?

What can you do to set yourself up for success ahead of a time you know you're likely to be triggered? If you want to be successful making better, conscious decisions, you'd better have a plan for how you're going to handle it when you encounter the things that prompt bad decisions or lead you to believe the lies that are getting in your way.

FIND THE LEVERAGE TO LIVE NO OTHER WAY

I'm sure you have a basic sense of what leverage is, this idea that the exerting of force from one thing helps create the result intended from another.

When it comes to pushing ourselves to grow into whoever we hope to become, the biggest reason we aren't already there is because we don't have a strong enough "why." I have been in this place many times. I had to feel stuck to appreciate that until I created urgency by creating a "why" that mattered enough to make me take action, I'd never really move. That's leverage.

It may be different for you, but from what I can tell from my past experiences, there are two types of leverage:

1. The kind that makes you think of how good things could be relative to how they are now, where by picturing that

future creates motivation for you to build a map to get from here to there.

2. The kind that makes you think how bad things could get relative to now if you don't get a handle on your life, how much you could lose if you were to keep heading down this mediocre road, or how bad you'd feel at the end of your life for not having fully lived.

I do think you need both, but I know that the second kind of leverage will force you to take dramatic action, immediately.

Let's start with the less effective but still important one first: painting a wildly specific, positive picture of what you're aiming for in your best-case scenario and being so detailed in the explanation of what it looks like that you can't help but get up and chase after it every single day. When you get into the nitty-gritty of the detail, you literally see yourself walking through life as that person you aspire to be, and the vision of that person acts as a catalyst to help you figure out how to get from here to there.

When you get so specific about the nuances of life, it begs bigger questions: What would it take for me to have these things in my life? If I want to become debt-free, then what do I need to do today to help me start down a path of financial freedom? If I want to have regular sex with my wife because we're in love like we were when we were first dating, what would I need to do today to reignite that spark? If I want to model the best way a man presents himself in the world to my boys when they're leaving for college, what do I need to do today as their dad to make sure they're being prepared well while they're still in elementary school?

Long before I left California, I visualized daily what the

Texas version of me would do and be relative to the LA version of me. I saw how I'd be in my untucked shirts with my sleeves rolled up, driving around in a badass vintage Bronco, going to the gym on the regular while being the dad who was able to have lunch with his kids at school a few times a month and the husband who's still actively dating his wife in a new city full of great food.

I painted a picture of the life I wanted to have, and that picture left bread crumbs for me to follow. The specifics of that picture helped me ask what action I'd need to take to make them come true. Trust me, I'm not all that special, but it did take work and focus. If you're willing to put in the work, if you're able to get detailed for what that chest-out swagger-machine looks like, and maybe most importantly, if you're able to create enough leverage, you can make your visualization come true too.

That said, painting a good picture isn't enough. At least it wasn't for me. In my world, I fell into a trap of comparing my best case with my good-enough case. And on the days when it felt hard to reach for more, I convinced myself it would be fine to just be fine. I negotiated with myself that, even though better was possible, I still had it pretty good, so I didn't need to put in the work. Yes, I might be in a funk, but my funk still left me better off than some of my friends or some of my family or someone born in rougher conditions.

I kept lowering the bar. I rationalized maintaining the status quo. I looked at how others in my circle had given up and used them to excuse myself from a higher standard, as if after a certain age or station in life, this was just as good as it got. I substituted gratitude for what I had for fully embracing the fruits that come from growth.

These things are not mutually exclusive.

You can be grateful for what you have and still want more.

You should be grateful for what you have and still want more.

Wanting more for your life doesn't come at the expense of what you already have. Wanting more for yourself allows you to better show up for what and who you already have in your life.

Which brings me to the other side of the leverage coin. For too long I'd convinced myself that the opposite of exceptional was okay. This is not true. The opposite of exceptional is miserable, and I hadn't fully tapped into the power of visualizing the worst-case scenario. While I tiptoed around being cool with mediocrity, I hadn't realized that the road I was on was actually leading toward misery if I didn't take dramatic action.

When my wife and I were sitting on our bed coming out of that ridiculous Hawaii trip, and she was laying it all out for me— that was me finally seeing the worst-case scenario. In a universe where I thought I could get by just getting by, Rachel articulated in a kind but direct way that if I were to maintain my trajectory, we would not be married in three years. She wasn't being a jerk about it. She was simply stating the facts. When I realized the truth of this, the very serious, worst-case scenario threat I was creating for our marriage became the strongest catalyst I could have ever imagined. It jolted me into wanting to make changes in my life. It pushed me into challenging my fixed mindset. It changed where my motivation was coming from. It helped me address my limiting beliefs. All those things happened when I started investing regularly in personal development, and in that personal development environment (in therapy, at conferences, in the pages of books) I was able to go much further into the dark side of leverage.

There I learned to come up with different variations of the future-you visualization: ones that are not about your best self but about your worst. In these exercises you picture what would happen if you were to allow yourself to keep believing the lies you've believed, to stay in the relationships that have held you back, to continue failing to support your kids and your spouse. Here you paint the picture of what it would mean to have your family fall apart if you aren't maniacal about boundaries with people of the opposite sex, how your health will fail you if you don't contain the drinking, how your kids will lose respect for you if you don't put down your technology. It's a dark exercise. It makes you feel, well, miserable. The opposite of exceptional. In this taste of misery, there's power.

I don't know what you struggle with, but since you're breathing, there's struggle. What I do know is, whatever you're struggling with, if you're don't think about the road you're heading down and acknowledge that it could end in misery, you're in trouble. If you think you're immune from your worst case, you may find it.

The bottom line about leverage: it's a very powerful tool for creating a "why" that's strong enough to move you from your current state to your future state. I recommend being exceptionally descriptive in coming up with your very best case and very worst case in a variety of categories in your life. When it comes to your health, your relationship with your partner, the way you parent, your faith, the way you provide, your legacy and impact on the world . . . do you know what you aspire to be through each lens? I don't mean generally, but in excruciating detail—do you know what you're aiming for in a way that draws a map you can follow to get there? At the same time, do you know the cost of not pursuing it?

That's leverage. Use those positive images as a map. Use those negative images to create the urgency you need to make massive change today. If your last day on earth was today, there'd be areas where you know you could do and be more. It's true for us all. The question now is, how can you create leverage to activate the change and turn the tide in those areas immediately?

BE DELIBERATE IN WHAT YOU FOCUS ON

You are what you focus on. Are you giving enough weight to that fact? Are you borderline crazy about building walls around your mind so you don't allow things in that slow your momentum or keep you from reaching as high as you might otherwise? If you're honest with yourself, have you really even given it thought? I hadn't. Not back when I felt stuck. While I was wondering why I couldn't get out of my funk, I was mindlessly focusing on and consuming things that wouldn't help me climb out of that ditch.

The first place I needed to start was my relationship with media.

The choices you make in how you spend your time and the relationship you have with media will inevitably influence the person you are. Whether you are a positive person or a negative person, a person who's full of hope or a person who's full of despair, a person who has anxiety or a person who feels confident about their future, many times it's a reflection of the kind of media you are consuming.

So how often are you truly thinking about what you consume, and how often are you considering how that consumption impacts your quality of life? Social media is a blessing and a curse. If you're measuring yourself or your relationships against the perfection others are advertising, chances are you won't feel great. If you are consuming a feed that tends to use language that's more negative than it is positive, that tends to be more abrasive than it is uplifting, the likelihood that you're going to walk into your life with a spirit of positivity, grace, or hope is much lower than if you consciously consider who you follow and what you allow in.

How many hours a week are you committing to screen time? If you are watching more than three hours of television every single night, you are choosing television as a priority over other things you could be doing to fuel your growth. That's not to say that sitting and enjoying a TV show here and there is bad, but when a screen is involved, you have to ask yourself how much it keeps you from conversation, community, learning, growing, or being challenged for more.

Porn. I just started a paragraph with the word *porn*, but guess what? Under the umbrella of media and what we consume, we've got to talk about it too. If you're not having an honest conversation about how pornography is influencing your thoughts, you're relinquishing your power to a force that will absolutely keep you from your best self. If you're in a relationship and this is a thing that lives in the dark as an unspoken secret, but you're still wondering why your sex life isn't what you'd hope it to be, don't be dumb. Porn is just too pervasive, and this can become an unbelievably huge barrier to the kind of intimacy you hope for and the kind of trust your relationship deserves. If you think that not talking about it or considering its impact serves you or your relationship in any way, think again.

It all comes down to balance and honestly evaluating how

our media consumption is fueling us or holding us back. Be honest about the trade-offs you make between the things you are making a priority right now and your relationships. Consider what impact that consumption is having on your state of mind, your demeanor, your sex drive, or whatever it might be.

If you're consuming negative things, you'll tend to be more negative, and it'll slow your growth and compromise your opportunities for fulfillment. If you're consuming more positive things, you'll tend to be a person who sees the world through a more positive lens—someone more motivated, more uplifting, and more effective. If you haven't already, do a thorough audit of what you consume by platform and by time. Don't let the fact that you've been consuming the same things for so long be the reason to not pay attention. If you want to chase the exceptional version of you, a deliberate, honest assessment of what you consume is a critically important foundational building block you have to address before you'll get anywhere.

If you're in a marriage that feels stuck and you can't figure out why, but you spend four hours a night watching television, now you know. You've prioritized television over intimacy. If you wish you could be more positive but spend half your day on Facebook in an argument about politics, now you know.

Beyond the focus on what you consume in media, let's talk health. Specifically, let's talk about what food you consume and how committed you are to exercise. For most of my life, I didn't make the full connection between making sound choices for my health and being able to unlock a richer life. Now, at forty-four, I not only see that very clear correlation but I also appreciate the responsibility I have as a father to model the kind of adult I want my four kids to become.

Is fast food still part of your life? If it is, I pass no judgment and encourage you to live your very best life, but . . . if you hope for bigger things, you have made a choice that comes at the expense of exceptional. Have you decided to believe a lie that this whole workout thing just isn't for you? If that's so, I pass no judgment and hope that the couch you're sitting on is as comfortable as possible, but . . . if you're not moving your body regularly, you've prioritized that couch of yours over an exceptional life. And yes, before you send your angry notes about me not understanding the hours that you work or the arthritis in your knees or your family of origin and how you're all big-boned, you need to hear loud and clear that if it were easy, everyone would be in great shape and eating well.

Yes, it's hard, but so is having a life that's fulfilling. Yes, it takes work, but that's what you're modeling to your kids. Yes, it requires mustering the strength to say yes to things you don't necessarily want to (daily workouts) or no to things you love (goodbye, apple fritters). I get you and your reasons, and I challenge you to get over them if you want to live a life worth living. It's hard to go to the gym every morning at 5:00 a.m. I do not like it one little bit. Especially when it's cold. Definitely not after the time change in winter. It's a drag to develop a new Friday-night habit after a lifetime of pizza delivery. I love pizza. I love chicken wings and breadsticks and the oversize chocolate chip cookie they offer to add on when you're already at the shopping cart online. But you know what I love more? Having the energy to play with my kids. You know what I love most? Having a body that's just a bit more in shape each day so that my wife is swatting my behind in a way that says, *We're totally having sex later*.

That said, hear this: this conversation about health isn't

about how you look or how much you weigh; it's about how you feel. How you feel is the foundation on top of which everything else is built.

From the time that I've spent with successful business leaders and the things I know of the ones I haven't met but admire from their books and podcasts, few things are as consistent among them all as a deliberate focus on what foods they consume and how they move their bodies. Commit to this as a focus, and you will see a fundamental change in so many other aspects of your life.

SURROUND YOURSELF WITH RELATIONSHIPS THAT SERVE YOU

When people tell me they're "stuck," one of the hardest exercises I recommend is to make a list of the people in their lives who don't support their next-level vision of themselves. I don't mean a biased "but they're family so they don't count" kind of summary; I mean a brutally honest list of who you're with the most and how their worldview, their ambition, their expertise, their limiting beliefs, their mindset, their motivation fuels you or impedes you. We've probably said it a thousand times on our daily live streams, echoing the sentiment of Jim Rohn and every other personal-development person it's been attributed to: "You are the five people you spend the most time with."[4] Please reread that sentence if you haven't heard it before. It's one of the simplest and most important concepts in this book and, though it may sound like common sense, if you haven't reviewed who you spend most of your time with lately, you're potentially getting in your own way without even knowing it by associating regularly with people who are holding you back.

Today is the day you need to start thinking differently about the way other people either push you to reach for more or act as an impediment to you becoming the very best version of yourself. We all have people who are inspirational and aspirational in our lives—if you don't, you need to find those people immediately and put them in regular rotation, even if they come in the form of podcasters and authors. And we all know people who believe that mediocrity is just their lot in life—that, as good as it is now, well, that's just as good as it gets for them. When you let the latter stick around, and they see you reaching for your version of more, their insecurity will make them work to keep you at their level so you don't expose them. These are people who have excuses for days, and their excuses are the platform they'll stand on to try and pull you back down. Not today, Satan.

How much are you thinking about your circle? How intentional are you about who you regularly surround yourself with? If you are the smartest person in your circle of five friends, you need a new circle. If you are the most driven person in your circle, you need a new circle. If you're the heathiest, happiest, in the strongest relationship, most positive . . . You. Need. A. New. Circle.

If you yield your power to people who don't have your destination in mind, you've ensured you won't get there. People who don't dream as big as you, who don't have as much hope for the future as you, who don't believe the exceptional life you're looking for is available—listening to those people will never help you get to where you want to go, and may very well keep you stuck, because you'll convince yourself that they're right. We all settle for just being okay sometimes.

Some people settle for mediocre.

But you choose whether to allow people who settle for a mediocre existence to be an important influence in your life. Choosing to eliminate people from your sphere of influence who hold you back will set you free.

You are on a mission toward a bigger and better version of you. You're following bread crumbs and reading the map you've created that guides you to where you're hoping to go. You need to put yourself into community with people who are doing things you respect, things you hope to emulate. You need a circle of people you might learn from, who will push you to grow.

And those people in your life who aren't going to help you get there? Those friends and family you've had in your life forever whom you'd struggle to shed? The goal isn't complete excommunication. You can still keep them in your life, but you need to do so with an explicit understanding that their presence and the influence you afford them are two totally different things. It's okay to have a beer with a buddy who's not driven, but it has to happen with an eyes-wide-open understanding that, while Brad may have been loads of fun to roll around town with in high school because he had that rad truck, he's not the guy you'll turn to when it comes to creating the life of your dreams. He's still telling stories about that truck, still wearing that flannel, still telling jokes you know aren't funny, and still waking up with a headache every day that he still won't attribute to being hungover. It's okay to relieve Brad of influence in your life.

And finally, relationships that serve you are not just about the relationships you have with other people. It's also about the relationship you have with yourself. With what you believe to be possible for yourself.

As much as my wife and I are known to say, "Hope is not a strategy," that doesn't discount the important power of hope for the future. Hope is an unbelievably important commodity. Do you have a hopeful vision of what your future looks like? Do you believe better times are ahead? Can you clearly see what the next-level version of you looks like, and does it light you up thinking about what it would mean to get there?

Les Brown famously said, "Hope for the future is power in the present." Good words.

If you don't have that vision, don't have that belief that better times are ahead, or can't see what the bigger version of you looks like, it likely means you haven't yet assigned the right value to the experiences of your past (Tony Robbins's idea of life happening for you versus to you) or are too anchored to the security that comes with the knowns of today versus the unknowns of tomorrow.[5]

The future that you aspire to will only come if you're willing to let go of what you need to release in your life today. What you know of your life today comes at the expense of what you're chasing for tomorrow. If you don't like change, you can't grow. If you like the comfort of today, you can't become who you're meant to be in the future.

So many times, we tend to perceive our need to change as a suggestion that we haven't been "right." You've been through all the "right" experiences you needed to get you this far and prepare you for what's ahead, but if you're going to get to where you want to be, you need to allow who you are or who you were to give way to who you're going to be. As long as you cling to either of those identities, you do so at the expense of giving yourself full permission to grow.

No matter what you do, change is coming, because change is a guarantee. If the fear of doing something new, because it produces something different, is the deterrent keeping you from starting this mission to a better you, well, friend, let that go. Your life is going to be different no matter what, so you might as well make it different in a way that serves you and those around you. Since you can't keep change from happening, embrace it, be more intentional with how you shape it, and see the differences that come as the good product of planning, discipline, and knowing where you're headed.

It is possible to get out of your own way, but it requires deliberate attention and careful coordination of many moving parts.

Are you going to accept this just-getting-by life? Are you going to be okay modeling so-so habits for your kids? Are you going to get to the end of your life and look back knowing that you did everything you could to create the very best experience for you and those in your orbit? That you worked hard to unlock every ounce of potential that your Creator gave you? Getting there requires committing today and every day to that bigger version of yourself that is inside you. For you. Forever.

It's been said, "Whether you think you can or think you can't, you're right." The choice is yours. Decide you can. Decide you will. Make the choice to reach for more.

Let's goooooo! The time is now. Get out of your own way.

RECOMMENDED READING

Brendon Burchard, *High Performance Habits: How Extraordinary People Become That Way* (Hay House Inc.)

Dr. Gary Chapman, *The 5 Love Languages: The Secret to Love That Lasts* (Northfield Publishing) and *When Sorry Isn't Enough: Making Things Right with Those You Love* (Northfield Publishing)

Jim Collins, *Good to Great: Why Some Companies Make the Leap and Others Don't* (HarperBusiness)

Stephen R. Covey, *The 7 Habits of Highly Effective People: Powerful Lessons in Personal Change* (Simon & Schuster)

Ray Dalio, *Principles: Life and Work* (Simon & Schuster)

Charles Duhigg, *The Power of Habit: Why We Do What We Do in Life and Business* (Random House)

Carol Dweck, *Mindset: The New Psychology of Success* (Random House)

Malcolm Gladwell, *The Tipping Point: How Little Things Can Make a Big Difference* (Back Bay Books)

Jen Hatmaker, *Interrupted: When Jesus Wrecks Your Comfortable Christianity* (NavPress)

Christopher L. Heuertz, *The Sacred Enneagram: Finding Your Unique Path to Spiritual Growth* (Zondervan)

Ryan Holiday, *The Obstacle Is the Way: The Timeless Art of Turning Trials into Triumph* (Portfolio)

Rachel Hollis, *Girl, Wash Your Face: Stop Believing the Lies About Who You Are So You Can Become Who You Were Meant to Be* (Thomas Nelson) and *Girl, Stop Apologizing: A Shame-Free Plan for Embracing and Achieving Your Goals* (HarperCollins Leadership)

Ben Horowitz, *The Hard Thing About Hard Things: Building a Business When There Are No Easy Answers* (HarperBusiness)

Robert Iger, *The Ride of a Lifetime: Lessons Learned from 15 Years as CEO of the Walt Disney Company* (Random House)

John C. Maxwell, *The 15 Invaluable Laws of Growth: Live Them and Reach Your Potential* (Center Street)

Patty McCord, *Powerful: Building a Culture of Freedom and Responsibility* (Silicon Guild)

Jack Mitchell, *Hug Your Customers: The Proven Way to Personalize Sales and Achieve Astounding Results* (Hachette Books)

Mel Robbins, *The 5 Second Rule: Transform Your Life, Work, and Confidence with Everyday Courage* (Savio Republic)

Sheryl Sandberg, *Lean In: Women, Work, and the Will to Lead* (Knopf)

Horst Schulze, *Excellence Wins: A No-Nonsense Guide to Becoming the Best in a World of Compromise* (Zondervan)

Kim Scott, *Radical Candor: Be a Kick-Ass Boss Without Losing Your Humanity* (St. Martin's Press)

Simon Sinek, *Leaders Eat Last: Why Some Teams Pull Together and Others Don't* (Portfolio)

ACKNOWLEDGMENTS

Thanks to you, reader, of all the books you could read, you chose this one and I don't take that lightly. Your support means the world.

To the community of humans who hang with us online, it means so much that so many of you have adopted me after having first followed Rachel. We're part of this very strange extended family and the support that you show me in buying this book or any of the things that we create at the Hollis Company has changed my life forever. A simple "thank you" doesn't go far enough in expressing my gratitude for the way you continue to show up for me, and us, every single day.

Thank you to the team at HarperCollins Leadership for the support they've provide this first-time author. Jeff James, Stephanie Tresner, Sara Broun, Sicily Axton, Hiram Centeno, and your teams—thank you so very much for all the support. To Tom Knight and the entire sales team—thank you for the effort with retail. To Jessica Wong and Brigitta Nortker—your edits hurt my feelings and made the book better, thank you. And to Brian Hampton—thank you for believing in me and for the support and friendship you offered to both me and Rachel. You are a good human who left us way too soon.

Thank you, Kevan Lyon, for the role you play both as literary agent and consigliere for all things publishing. You make me so much smarter.

Thank you to the Walt Disney Company for the almost two decades of support. To the leadership across the company—your championing of my past life and belief in me as a leader is an indelible part of who I am. To the teams I was fortunate enough to lead and the support teams that surrounded me—thank you for working so hard that any of my shortcomings and inexperience were blurred away. I'll forever be grateful to the greatness of the Walt Disney Company and its extraordinary people who were complicit in my jump to the adventure of the rest of my life.

Thank you to the entire team at the Hollis Company for braving the last eighteen months. You've made it all look so easy: the launch of books, digital education, live events, a documentary, new podcasts, a clothing line, a new retail partner, and all the things. The ability to thrive in a short window where we grew from four to sixty employees is not only an extraordinary feat in and of itself, but that you were able to do so against the backdrop of my adjusting to small-business life and the emotional roller coaster of this book is a testament to each of you as the leaders we need for the future. Thank you for your steady hand in the chaotic, choppy seas of growth. This is just the beginning. I can't wait to see all we'll build together.

To my parents—thank you for always being there for me, for your unconditional love, for the values you instilled in me. I love you. I am the man, husband, and father I am today because of your model. Heather and Chuck, Andy and Erin, Tim and Kirsten and all of your 1,000 kids—I love you and appreciate the way that you've been a support to me through the years. Farrell,

Sheree, Christina, Melody, and your families—I love you and thank you for bringing me in and loving me as one of your own.

Jackson Cage, Sawyer Neeley, Ford Baker, and Noah Elizabeth —being your father is among the greatest accomplishments of my lifetime. I'll work every day to equip you with the tools to navigate around your own pitfalls and work even harder to make you proud. I love you each more than I could ever fully express. Thank you for being such an important piece of my "why."

And to my best friend, Rachel, I just love you so very much. You astound me with the woman you continue to grow into. Your belief in what is possible for your life made me believe in things I didn't think possible for my own. Your pursuit of continual growth acts as an inspiration for my own uneasy climb. Your superpowers of accountability are the worst and some of the most important skills you bring to this partnership. Thank you for making me laugh. Thank you for your support through this work transition and the book writing and choosing to love me every day—especially on the days as people running a business together where love was very much a choice. Thank you for the attention you've paid to arm workouts and the small divots that have become part of our family as a testament to your hard work. Thank you for entrusting me with leading this team beside you. Words can't express how excited I am for the work we'll do together. I don't know so many things, but I do know this: I'll struggle the rest of my life trying to figure out how to hold my pride for your accomplishments and my gratitude for your love since both on their own are more than most could carry. Let's go change the world.

I thank God every day that I was afforded these blessings, the gift of these gifts, and the chance to get out of my own way to fully use what I've been given for good.

NOTES

INTRODUCTION

1. Robert Frost, *A Boy's Will and North of Boston* (Mineola, NY: Dover Publications, 2012), loc. 2036 of 3162, Kindle.

CHAPTER 4: A DRINK WILL MAKE THIS BETTER

1. John C. Maxwell, *The 15 Invaluable Laws of Growth* (New York: Center Street, 2012), 126.

CHAPTER 5: I DID SOMETHING WRONG, SO I AM SOMETHING WRONG

1. Brené Brown, "Listening to Shame," March 2012, TED.com, video, 20:31, https://www.ted.com/talks/brene_brown_listening_to_shame.
2. *Super Soul Sunday*, "Brené Brown: Vulnerability Is the Key to Unlocking Intimacy," aired March 2013, on OWN, http://www .oprah.com/own-super-soul-sunday/brene-brown-why-being -vulnerable-is-the-key-to-unlocking-intimacy.

CHAPTER 6: EVERYONE IS THINKING ABOUT WHAT I'M DOING

1. Bennett Cerf, *Shake Well Before Using: A New Collection of Impressions and Anecdotes Mostly Humorous* (New York: Simon & Schuster, 1948), 249.

CHAPTER 8: FAILURE MEANS YOU'RE WEAK

1. Carol S. Dweck, *Mindset: The New Psychology of Success* (New York: Ballantine Books, 2007).
2. John Shedd, *Salt from My Attic* (Portland, ME: Mosher Press, 1928).

CHAPTER 13: I KNOW WHAT SHE NEEDS

1. Rachel Hollis and Dave Hollis, "Conflict Resolution, Enneagram Number and How Knowing Both Can Change Your Relationship," August 31, 2018, in *Rise Together*, podcast, episode 8, MP3 audio, 61:00, https://www.risetogetherpodcast.com/episodes/2018/8/23/conflict-resolution-personality-type.
2. Hollis and Hollis, "The Five Love Languages with Dr. Gary Chapman," January 16, 2019, in *Rise Together*, podcast, episode 29, MP3 audio, 42:00, https://podcasts.apple.com/us/podcast/29-the-five-love-languages-with-dr-gary-chapman/id1407481308?i=1000429480755.

CHAPTER 14: MY ROLE IN THIS RELATIONSHIP IS CONSTANT

1. Kim Scott, *Radical Candor: Be a Kick-Ass Boss Without Losing Your Humanity* (New York: St. Martin's Press, 2017).

CHAPTER 16: I KNOW WHAT YOU'VE BEEN THROUGH

1. PJ Voigt and Alex Goldman, "Raising the Bar," January 21, 2016, in *Reply All*, podcast, episode 52, MP3 audio, 37:45, https://gimletmedia.com/shows/reply-all/76h54l.

CHAPTER 17: THINGS THAT ARE POSSIBLE FOR OTHER PEOPLE AREN'T POSSIBLE FOR ME

1. Michael Rothman, "Amy Purdy Reveals Why She Has an Advantage on 'Dancing with the Stars,'" ABC News, March 19, 2014, https://abcnews.go.com/Entertainment/amy-purdy-reveals-advantage-dancing-stars/story?id=22967243.

BONUS CHAPTER: MENTAL HEALTH ISN'T AS IMPORTANT AS PHYSICAL HEALTH

1. "Mental Health Information," National Institute of Mental Health, https://www.nimh.nih.gov/health/statistics/mental-illness.shtml.
2. "5 Surprising Mental Health Statistics," Mental Health First Aid, https://www.mentalhealthfirstaid.org/2019/02/5-surprising-mental-health-statistics/.

CONCLUSION

1. William Yardley, "Zig Ziglar, Motivational Speaker, Dies at 86," *New York Times*, November 28, 2012, https://www.nytimes.com/2012/11/29/business/zig-ziglar-86-motivational-speaker-and-author.html.
2. Jeffrey Kluger, "Why You're Pretty Much Unconscious All the Time," *Time*, June 26, 2015, https://time.com/3937351/consciousness-unconsciousness-brain/.
3. Charles Duhigg, *The Power of Habit: Why We Do What We Do in Life and Business* (New York: Random House, 2014).
4. Jim Rohn, *The Art of Exceptional Living* (Chicago: Nightingale-Conant, 1993).
5. "Life Is Happening for Me," *The Tony Robbins Blog*, TonyRobbins.com, accessed October 5, 2019, https://www.tonyrobbins.com/mind-meaning/life-is-happening-for-me/.

ABOUT THE AUTHOR

Dave Hollis is CEO of the Hollis Company, a company built around the belief that everybody is made for more, with the intention of putting tools in people's hands to help them build better lives. He is husband to Rachel and father to Jackson, Sawyer, Ford, and Noah. Together with his wife, Dave hosts *The Start Today Morning Show* (the morning show that no one is talking about) and the podcast *Rise Together*, the number one health podcast on iTunes. Dave was previously president of distribution for Walt Disney Studios until he left to apply his experiences to the expansion of the Hollis Company. Dave is a member of the Motion Picture Academy and has served as an advisor or board member of technology incubator Fandango Labs; philanthropy start-up Givsum; film charity Will Rogers Pioneers Foundation; his alma mater Pepperdine's Institute for Entertainment, Media, Sports, and Culture; and foster care champion National Angels. Dave and his family live in Austin, Texas, where he's an avid sports fan, drives a 1969 Ford Bronco named Incredible Hulk, and has a mini schnauzer named Jeffrey.